FamilyCircle

easyTOYS

FamilyCircle®
*easy*TOYS

25 Delightful Creations to Knit and Crochet

sixth&spring books
New York

Sixth&Spring Books
233 Spring Street
New York, NY 10013

Editorial Director
Trisha Malcolm

Art Director
Chi Ling Moy

Book Manager
Shannon Kerner

Instructions Writer
Louisa Cameron-Smith

Stylist
Mary Hampton Helt

Copy Writer
Miriam Gold

Proofreader
Jean Guirguis

Yarn Editor
Veronica Manno

Technical Editors
Carla Scott
Pat Harste

President and Publisher, Sixth&Spring Books
Art Joinnides

Family Circle Magazine
Editor-in-Chief
Susan Kelliher Ungaro

Executive Editor
Barbara Winkler

Creative Director
Diane Lamphron

Photo credits:
Scott Cameron
Pages 59, 63, 81, 85

Jack Deutsch
Pages 43, 44

Dan Howell
Pages 2,9, 15, 17, 20, 24, 26, 29, 30, 36, 40, 47, 48, 50, 55, 57, 65, 66, 72, 75, 77, 92, 94, 97, 100, 105, 107, 109, 112, 114, 116, 118, 119, 120, 121, 128

Peter Kooijman/Sanoma Syndication
Pages 39, 97

Rudy Molacek
Pages 6, 33

Nick Vacarro
Page 69

Marco Zambelli
Pages 7, 87, 88

Manufactured in China

1 3 5 7 9 8 6 4 2

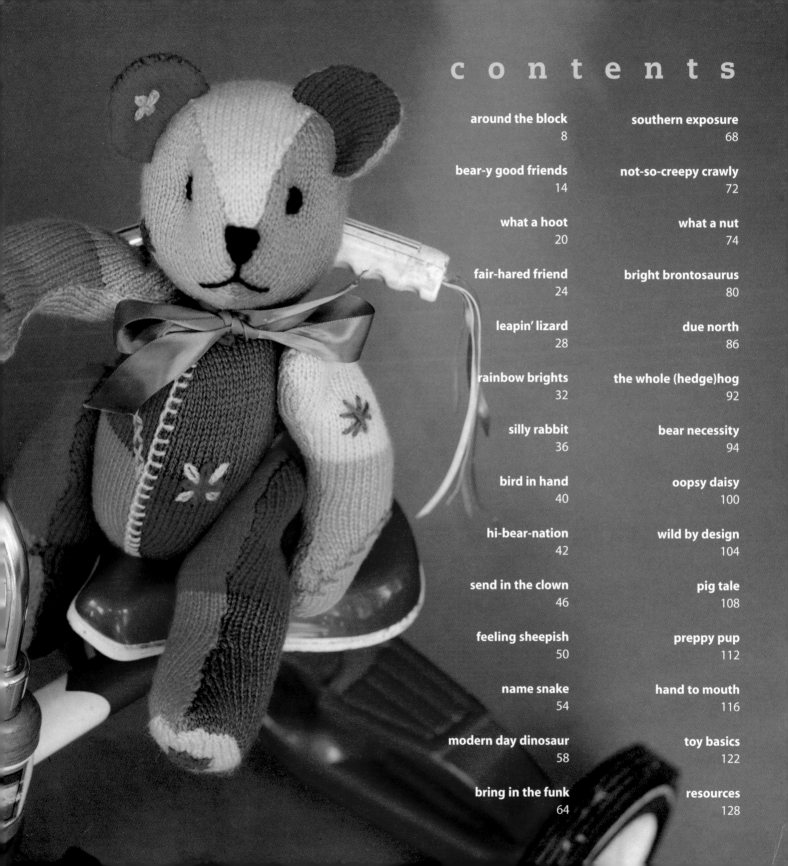

contents

introduction

In this day and age when video games, electronic gadgets and DVDs seem to be children's entertainment of choice, the idea of handknitted playthings almost seems obsolete. After all, there are no lights, no sound, no action; where's the thrill?

But just as kids need to be stimulated and excited, they also need calm downtime to develop their imaginations, establish a respect for learning, and enjoy tactile contact with the world around them. With their quirky characteristics, colors and fibers, knitted toys give them a chance to do all three. Projects such as "Around the Block" will spark their interest in shapes and letters, while others like "Rainbow Brights" will trigger an appreciation for color. Then there is our marvelous menagerie—pandas and reptiles included—guaranteed to pique any child's interest.

That's not to say that only little ones benefit from a good knitted toy. The time and skill that goes into these fantastic projects are priceless and satisfying, not to mention the love and pride you'll glean from creating them. As you flip through the following pages, try those patterns that will inspire you and youngsters alike. The end results, from new interests to cherished possessions, may surprise you.

Take a humble cube from dull to dynamic with this vivid quick knit that teaches color and shape as well as the alphabet to toddlers. Six squares are joined with a crochet chain for simple construction, while contrast duplicate stitching completes the project.

a r o u n d   t h e   b l o c k

materials
Cotton Classic by Tahki
Yarns/Tahki•Stacy Charles, Inc.,
1¾ oz/50g balls, each approx
108yds/97m (cotton)
1 ball each in #3401 Orange (A), #3533
Yellow (B), #3871 Blue (C), #3726 Lime
Green, #3924 Purple (E), #3458 Pink (F)
and #3488 Red (G)
One pair size 6 (4mm) needles
OR SIZE TO OBTAIN GAUGE
Size G/6 (4mm) crochet hook
Yarn needle
Foam rubber cut into 3"/7.5cm cubes

FINISHED MEASUREMENTS

3" x 3" x 3"/7.5cm x 7.5cm x 7.5cm

GAUGE

24 sts and 28 rows to 4"/10cm over St st using size 6 (4mm) needles.

TAKE TIME TO CHECK YOUR GAUGE

NOTES

Each block consists of 6 squares. Shapes and letters are embroidered with duplicate st (using strongly contrasting colors) on 4 sides of the block, with letters on 2 opposite sides and shapes on other 2 sides.

Top and bottom squares are made in same color as yarn used for joining and are left blank. Join squares with single crochet.

BLOCK

Square (make 6). Cast on 17 sts. Work in St st for 20 rows. Bind off.

Continued on page 10

Designed by Darlene Hayes

around the block

Continued from page 8

FINISHING

Apply letters and shapes to 4 of the squares using duplicate st, and following charts. In the samples, 1 letter and 1 shape were used for a single block.

Weave in loose yarn ends. Take 2 squares and with WS tog, join with sc. Join 2 more squares so that you have a row of 4 attached to one another. Join the first square to the last square. Take one of the 2 rem squares and join it to the bottom edges of the 4 previously joined squares. Join 2 sides of the last square to the top. Insert a foam cube then join the rem 2 sides. Weave in all the loose yarn ends, using the leftover tails to make an unbroken line of sts at the corners if necessary.

Charts continue on page 12

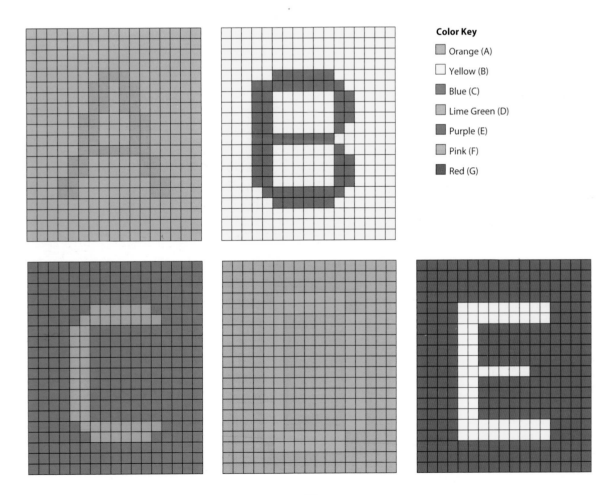

Color Key

☐ Orange (A)

☐ Yellow (B)

☐ Blue (C)

☐ Lime Green (D)

☐ Purple (E)

☐ Pink (F)

☐ Red (G)

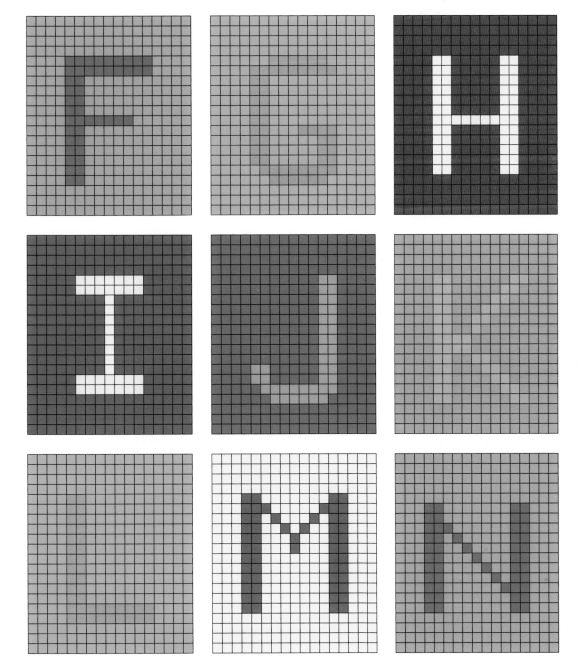

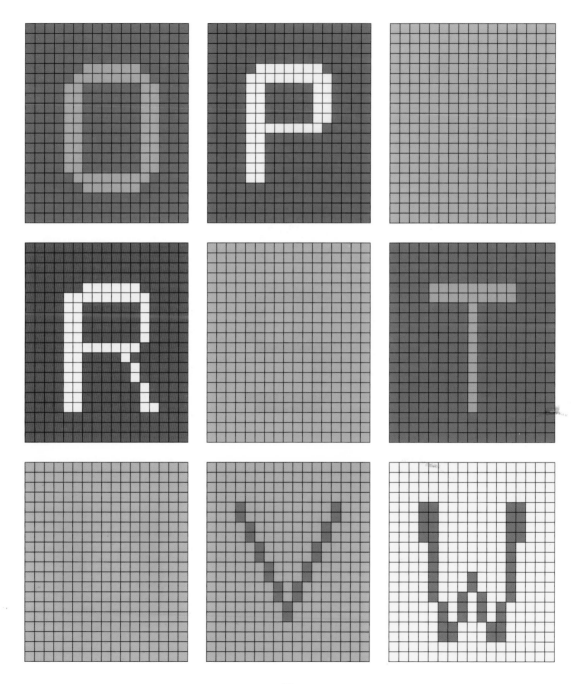

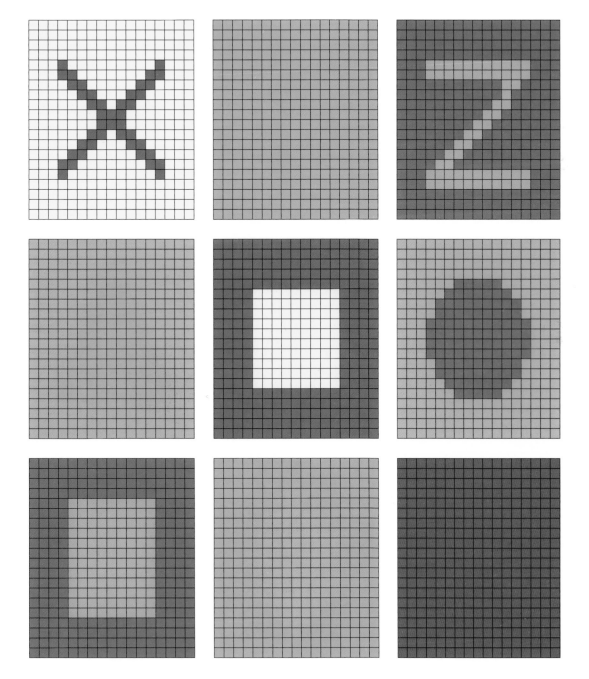

Who can resist the sweetness of a classic Teddy? Featuring button-jointed limbs for easy movement and softly textured yarn for a down-home vintage look, this super-size snuggler is the perfect buddy.

bear-y good friends

materials

Alpaca Bouclé by
Indiecita/Plymouth Yarns
1½oz/50g each approx 70yds/63m
(alpaca/nylon)
25 balls #13 Dk Brown
One pair size 11 (8mm) needles
OR SIZE TO OBTAIN GAUGE
Stitch markers and holders
Small amount of smooth
yarn for sewing
Small amount black embroidery floss
Four 1"/25mm brown buttons
Two ¾"/20mm black shank
buttons for eyes
Fiberfill
Yarn needle

Designed by Jenny Bellew

FINISHED MEASUREMENTS

Approx 34"/86cm tall.

GAUGE

12 sts and 14 rows to 4"/10cm over rev St st using size 11 (8mm) needles and 2 strands of yarn held tog.

TAKE TIME TO CHECK YOUR GAUGE.

NOTE

Work with 2 strands of yarn held tog throughout.

BODY BACK

Cast on 4 sts.

Row 1 (RS) Knit, inc 1 in each st across—8 sts.

Row 2 P3, [inc in next st] twice, p3.

Row 3 Inc in first st, k3, [inc in next st] twice, k3, inc in last st.

Row 4 P6, [inc in next st] twice, p6.

Row 5 K7, [inc in next st] twice, k7.

Row 6 P8, [inc in next st] twice, p8.

Row 7 Inc in first st, k8, [inc in next st] twice, k8, inc in last st—24 sts.

Row 8 and all WS rows Purl.

Row 9 K11, [inc in next st] twice, k11.

Continued on page 16

bear-y good friends

Continued from page 14

Row 11 Inc in first st, k11, [inc in next st] twice, k11, inc in last st.

Row 13 K14, [inc in next st] twice, k14.

Row 15 Inc in first st, k14, [inc in next st] twice, k14, inc in last st.

Row 17 K17, [inc in next st] twice, k17.

Row 19 Inc in first st, k17, [inc in next st] twice, k17, inc in last st—42 sts.

Work in St st for 3 rows.

Next row (RS) Inc in first st, k19, [inc in next st] twice, k19, inc in last st. Cont in St st, inc 1 st each side every 4th row twice—50 sts. Work even in St st for 6 rows. Cont in St st, dec 1 st each side every 4th row 4 times—42 sts.

Next row P19, [p2tog] twice, p19.

Next row K18, [k2tog] twice, k18.

Next row P17, [p2tog] twice, p17.

Next row K2tog, k14, [k2tog] twice, k14, k2tog.

Next row P14, [p2tog] twice, p14.

Next row K13, [k2tog] twice, k13.

Next row P12, [p2tog] twice, p12.

Next row K2tog, k9, [k2tog] twice, k9, k2tog.

Next row P2tog, p7, [k2tog] twice, p7, p2tog.

Bind off rem 18 sts.

FRONT

Cast on 4 sts.

Row 1 Knit.

Row 2 and all WS rows Purl.

Row 3 Knit, inc 1 in each st across—8 sts.

Row 5 K3, [inc in next st] twice, k3.

Row 7 Inc in first st, k3, [inc in next st] twice, k3, inc in last st.

Row 9 K6, [inc in next st] twice, k6.

Row 11 Inc in first st, k6, [inc in next st] twice, k6, inc in last st. Cont incs as established, alternating 2 incs with 4 incs, until there are 50 sts. Work 3 rows even, inc 1 st each side of next row—52 sts. Work 7 rows even.

Next row K2tog, k22, [k2tog] twice, k22, k2tog. Work 3 rows even.

Next row K2tog, k20, [k2tog] twice, k20, k2tog. Work 3 rows even.

Next row K2tog, k18, [k2tog] twice, k18, k2tog. Work 3 rows even.

Next row K2tog, k16, [k2tog] twice, k16, k2tog. Work 1 row even.

Next row K16, [k2tog] twice, k16. Work 1 row even.

Next row K2tog, k13, [k2tog] twice, k13, k2tog. Work 1 row even.

Next row K13, [k2tog] twice, k13. Work 1 row even.

Next row K2tog, k10, [k2tog] twice, k10, k2tog.

Next row P2tog, p8, [k2tog] twice, p8, p2tog.

Bind off rem 20 sts.

HEAD

Right side Cast on 18 sts. Beg with a knit row, work in St st for 2 rows.

Row 3 K, inc 1 st each side.

Rows 4 and 6 Purl.

Row 5 K, inc 1 st in last st.

Row 7 Inc 1 in first st, k to end.

Row 8 Cast on 2 sts, p to end—24 sts.

Row 9 Knit.

Row 10 Rep row 8. Rep last 4 rows twice— 36 sts.

Next row Rep row 7. Work 2 rows even. Bind off

2 sts at beg of next row—35 sts. Dec 1 st at end of next row. Work 1 row even. Rep last 2 rows 3 more times—31 sts. Work 1 row even. Dec 1 st each side of next row, then every other row until 9 sts rem. Bind off.

Left side Work as for right side, reversing shaping.

GUSSET

Cast on 7 sts. Work in St st for 4 rows, inc 1 st each side of next row, then every 6th row until 21 sts. Work 5 rows even. Dec 1 st each side of next row, then dec 1 each side every 4th row 6 times, then every other row twice—3 sts. Work 1 row even.

Next row K1, k2tog.

Next row P2tog, fasten off.

EARS (MAKE 2)

Cast on 18 sts. Work in St st for 8 rows. Dec 1 st each side every other row 3 times, every row 3 times—6 sts. Work 2 rows even. Inc 1 st each side every row 3 times, every other row 3 times—18 sts. Work 7 rows even. Bind off.

ARMS

Left half (Make 2) Cast on 2 sts. K 1 row, inc 1 st each side.

Next row Inc in first st, p to end.

Next row K, inc 1 st each side. Rep last 2 rows twice—13 sts. Cont in St st, inc 1 st at end of every WS row 3 times. Work 1 row even.

Next row K2tog, k to last st, inc in last st.

Next row Purl. Rep last 2 rows 4 times—16 sts. Work 6 rows even. Inc 1 st at beg of next and foll 4th row—18 sts. Work 3 rows even.

Next row Inc in first st, k to last 2 sts, k2tog. Rep last 4 rows 5 times—18 sts. Work 1 row even. Cont in St st, dec 1 st each side every row 6 times. Bind off rem 6 sts.

Right half (Make 2) Work as for left half, reversing shaping.

LEGS

Left half (Make 2) Cast on 26 sts. Work in St st for 2 rows. Dec 1 st at end of next row, then 1 st at same edge every row 4 times more, then every other row twice, every 4th row twice—17 sts. Work 5 rows even. Inc 1 st each side of next row—19 sts. Work 5 rows even.

Next row Inc 1 st each side. Work 5 rows even. Rep last inc row—23 sts. Work 5 rows even. Dec 1 st each side next row, then every 4th row once, every other row twice, every row 5 times. Bind off rem 5 sts.

bear-y good friends

Continued from page 17

Right half (Make 2) Work as for left half, reversing shaping.

Sole (Make 2) Cast on 4 sts. Work in St st for 2 rows. Cast on 2 sts at beg of next 2 rows, inc 1 st each side every row twice—12 sts. Work 14 rows even. Dec 1 st each side every other row twice, every row 3 times.

Next row K2tog, fasten off.

FINISHING

Note Use smooth yarn for sewing. Foll diagram, join left and right head pieces tog from neck to tip of nose. Sew head gusset between head pieces so that gusset ends at tip of nose, leave neck edge open. Join front and back body pieces, leaving neck edge open. Sew pairs of arms tog, leaving an opening for stuffing. Firmly stuff body, head and arms. Sew arm openings closed. Sew pairs of legs tog, stuff, sew sole to bottom of foot. With 6 strands of floss, embroider mouth and nose in straight st. Sew on eyes. Sew head to body, adding additional stuffing if necessary to make neck firm. Fold ears in half and sew side seams, then sew to head. Foll diagram, attach arms and legs by stitching through button, then through arm or leg, bear body, rem arm or leg, then 2nd button.

HOW TO ASSEMBLE BEAR

Joining head pieces

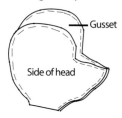

Gusset

Side of head

Attaching limbs

Joining leg pieces

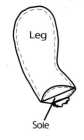

Leg

Sole

This charming project proves that the wise old owl can be adorable as well. Worked in novelty fiber for a feathery, two-tone effect, this brainy bird also features crocheted claws and duplicate-stitch detailing.

what a hoot

materials
Boa by Bernat, 1¾oz/50g balls, each approx 71yds/64m (polyester)
2 balls in #81044 Swan (MC) and 1 ball each in #81005 Dove (A) and #81042 Ostrich (B)
Satin by Bernat, 1¾oz/50g balls, each approx 71yds/64m (acrylic)
1 ball in #04046 Sterling (C) and 2yds in #04040 Ebony (D)
One pair each sizes 5 and 7 (3.75 and 4.5mm) needles
OR SIZE TO OBTAIN GAUGE
Size E/5 (3.75mm) crochet hook
Fiberfill
2 eye buttons
Yarn needle

Designed by Svetlana Avrakh

FINISHED MEASUREMENTS
14"/35.5cm tall

GAUGE
20 sts and 26 rows to 4"/10cm over rev St st with MC using size 7 (4.5mm) needles. TAKE TIME TO CHECK YOUR GAUGE.

BODY
With larger needles and MC, cast on 32 sts.

Row 1 (RS) Purl.

Row 2 and all WS rows Knit.

Row 3 (RS) P1, [inc 1 st in next st, p3] 7 times, inc 1 st in next st, p2—40 sts.

Row 5 P2, [inc 1 st in next st, p4] 7 times, inc 1 st in next st, p2—48 sts. Work 5 rows even in rev St st.

Next row (RS) P15, inc 1 st in next st, p to last 16 sts, inc 1 st in next st, p15.

Next row Knit. Rep last 2 rows 3 times more—56 sts.

Next row (RS) P13, *inc 1 st in next st, p1, inc 1 st in next st*, p to last 16 sts, rep from * to * once, p13.

Next row Knit. Rep last 2 rows twice more—68 sts. Work 24 rows even.

Dec Row 1 (RS) P17, p2tog, p to last 19 sts, ssp, p17. Rep Dec Row 1 every

Continued on page 22

what a hoot

Continued from page 21

other row 3 times more—60 sts.

Dec Row 2 (WS) K17, SKP, k to last 19 sts, k2tog, k17. Rep Dec Rows 1 and 2 twice more, then work Dec Row 1 once—48 sts.

HEAD

Next row (WS) Join A and knit, inc 7 sts evenly across—55 sts.

Next row (RS) Knit. Cont in St st for 29 rows more. Break A, leaving a long end. Thread yarn through all sts, pull tog tightly and fasten securely.

HEAD COVERING

With RS facing, larger needles and B, pick up and k55 sts evenly along first A row of head.

Next row (WS) Knit.

Right section *Row 1 (RS)* With MC, p22, turn work leaving rem 33 sts on a holder.

Row 2 (WS) K2tog, k to end—21 sts.

Row 3 With B, p to last 2 sts, p2tog—20 sts.

Row 4 and all foll WS rows Knit with color of preceding row.

Row 5 With MC, p to last 2 sts, p2tog—19 sts.

Row 7 With B, purl.

Row 9 With MC, purl.

Row 11 With B, p to last 2 sts, inc 1 st in next st, p1.

Row 12 Knit.

Rows 13 and 14 With MC, rep rows 11 and 12.

Rep rows 11-14 twice more, then rows 11 and 12 once—26 sts. Break MC and B. Place sts on a st holder.

Center section Place 33 sts from st holder onto larger needle, ready to work a RS row.

Row 1 (RS) With B, ssp, p7, p2tog, place rem 22 sts on a holder.

Row 2 Knit.

Row 3 Ssp, p to last 2 sts, p2tog. Rep rows 2 and 3 twice more—3 sts. Work 5 rows even.

Next row (RS) [Inc 1 st in next st] twice, p1—5 sts.

Next row Knit.

Next row Inc 1 st in first st, p2, inc 1 st in next st, p1—7 sts. Work 5 rows even. Break B and place sts on a st holder.

Left section Place rem 22 sts onto larger needle, ready to work a RS row.

Row 1 (RS) With MC, p22.

Row 2 (WS) K to last 2 sts, SKP—21 sts.

Row 3 With B, ssp, p to end—20 sts.

Row 4 and all foll WS rows Knit with color of preceding row.

Row 5 With MC, ssp, p to end—19 sts.

Row 7 With B, purl.

Row 9 With MC, purl.

Row 11 With B, inc 1 st in first st, p to end.

Row 12 Knit.

Rows 13 and 14 With MC, rep rows 11 and 12.

Rep rows 11-14 twice more, then rows 11 and 12 once—26 sts. Break MC and B. Place sts on a st holder.

Join sections Sl sts of all 3 sections onto larger needle, ready to work a RS row.

Row 1 (RS) With MC, p26 from right section, p7 from center section, p26 from left section—59 sts.

Rows 2, 4, 6, 8 and 10 Knit.

Rows 3 and 7 With B, purl.

Rows 5 and 9 With MC, purl. Break MC. Break B, leaving a long end. Thread yarn through rem sts and tighten up. Fasten securely. Sew back seam of body, head and head covering, stuffing head and body before closing up seam.

RIGHT WING

Note When changing colors, twist yarns on WS to prevent holes in the work.

With larger needles and A, cast on 5 sts (inside of wing), then with MC, cast on 5 sts (outside)—10 sts.

Row 1 (RS) K5 MC; k5 A.

Row 2 and all WS rows Purl, matching colors.

Row 3 With MC, k4, inc 1 st in next st; with A, inc 1 st in next st, k4.

Row 5 With MC, inc 1 st in first st, k to 1 st before center, inc 1 st in next st; with A, inc 1 st in next st, k to last 2 sts, inc 1 st in next st, k1.

Row 7 With MC, k to 1 st before center, inc 1 st in next st; with A, inc 1 st in next st, k to end.

Row 8 Purl, matching colors.

Rows 9-20 Rep rows 5-8 three times—36 sts.

Row 21 With B, inc 1 st in first st, k to center; with A, k to last 2 sts, inc 1 st in next st, k1.

Rows 22 and 24 Purl, matching colors.

Row 23 With MC, k to center; with A, k to end.

Rows 25-40 Rep rows 21-24 four times—46 sts.

Row 41 With B, k to center; with A, k to end.

Rows 42 and 44 Purl, matching colors.

Row 43 With MC, k to center; with A, k to end.

Rows 45-50 Rep rows 41-44 once, then rows 41 and 42 once more. Bind off. Fold wing in half and sew side, top and bottom seams.

LEFT WING

With larger needles and MC, cast on 5 sts (outside of wing), then with A, cast on 5 sts (inside)—10 sts. Work as for right wing, switching colors. Sew wings on body.

TAIL

With B, cast on 35 sts. P 1 row, k 1 row. With MC, p 1 row, k 1 row. Break MC.

Next row (RS) With B, p1, [p2tog, p12, p2tog, p1] twice—31 sts.

Next row Knit.

Next row Sl first 8 sts to RH needle, re-join MC and p15, turn work, leaving rem 8 sts unworked.

Next row (WS) With MC, k17, sl rem 6 sts to RH needle.

Next row With B, p1, [p2tog, p10, p2tog, p1] twice—27 sts.

Next row Knit.

Next row Sl first 7 sts to RH needle, with MC, p13, turn work, leaving rem 7 sts unworked.

Next row (WS) With MC, k15, sl rem 5 sts to RH needle.

Next row With B, p1, [p2tog, p8, p2tog, p1] twice—23 sts.

Next row Knit. With MC, p 1 row, k 1 row. Break MC. With B, p1, [inc 1 st in next st, p8, inc 1 st in next st, p1] twice—27 sts.

Next row Knit.

Next row (RS) Sl first 7 sts to RH needle, join MC and p5, inc 1 st in next st, p1, inc 1 st in next st, p5, turn work, leaving rem 7 sts unworked.

Next row (WS) With MC, k15, sl rem 7 sts to RH needle.

Next row With B, p1, [inc 1 st in next st, p11, inc 1 st in next st, p1] twice—33 sts.

Next row Knit.

Next row (RS) Sl first 8 sts to RH needle, then with MC, p17, turn work, leaving rem 8 sts unworked.

Next row (WS) With MC, k16, sl rem 9 sts to RH needle. Break MC.

Next row With B, p1, [inc 1 st in next st, p13, inc 1 st in next st, p1] twice—37 sts.

Next row Knit. Join MC and p 1 row, k 1 row. Bind off. Fold tail in half. Sew side edges tog. Sew top and bottom edges. Sew tail on body.

LEGS (MAKE 2)

With smaller needles and C, cast on 21 sts. Work 18 rows in St st. Bind off. Fold leg in half widthwise and sew side and top seam.

CLAWS

With RS facing, crochet hook and D, join yarn in first st at top right side of paw, [ch 4, work sl st in same st, work long sc approx $1/4$"/.5cm from sl st] 3 times, ch 4, work sl st in same st. Fasten off. Stuff legs and attach to body. With yarn needle and D, work several long sts on center of head covering for beak (see photo). Sew on eyes. Sew short lengths of B around eyes for lashes.

Bring a beguiling backyard favorite to the toy chest with this floppy-eared, bushy-tailed plushie made with delicate-yet-nubbly yarn. The faux-gingham lining adds an authentic rustic touch, and his kindly features are finished with a little elementary embroidery.

fair-hared friend

materials
Baby Teri by Red Heart®/Coats & Clark,
3oz/85g balls, each approx
200yds/180m (acrylic/nylon)
2 balls in #9181 Blue (MC)
TLC Baby by Red Heart®/Coats & Clark,
6oz/170g balls, each approx
509yds/458m (acrylic)
Small amounts each of
#5011 White (A),
#5881 Powder Blue (B), and
#7812 Sky Blue (C)
1yd/1m each of soft pink and taupe
yarn for embroidering face and paws
One pair each sizes 6 and 10½
(4 and 6.5mm) needles
OR SIZE TO OBTAIN GAUGE
Stitch holders and markers
Fiberfill
Yarn needle for embroidery

Designed by Gayle Bunn

FINISHED MEASUREMENTS

Approx 14"/35.5cm long

GAUGE

12 sts and 20 rows to 4"/10cm over St st with 2 strands of MC held together using size 10½ (6.5mm) needles.

TAKE TIME TO CHECK YOUR GAUGE.

NOTE

Work with 2 strands of MC held tog throughout.

UPPER BODY

With larger needles and 2 strands MC, cast on 36 sts. Place markers each side of row. Work 2 rows in St st.

Shape back legs *Inc row (RS)* K1, M1, k to last st, M1, k1. Work 1 row even. Rep last 2 rows 5 times more—48 sts.

Right back leg *Next row (RS)* K8, place rem 40 sts on a holder. Work first 8 sts as foll: Work 3 rows even in St st. Dec 1 st each side on next row. Work 1 row even. Rep last 2 rows once more. Bind off rem 4 sts.

Center of body Place 40 sts from holder onto needle, ready to work a RS row. Join MC and work as foll:

Next row (RS) Bind off 1 st, k to last 9 sts, place last 9 sts on a holder for left back leg. Work 7 rows in St st on 30 sts.

Continued on page 26

25

f a i r - h a r e d   f r i e n d

Continued from page 25

Shape front legs *Inc row (RS)* K1, M1, k to last st, M1, k1. Work 1 row even. Rep last 2 rows 5 times more—42 sts. K1, M1, k11, bind off next 18 sts, k to last st, M1, k1. Cont on last 13 sts only.

Left front leg *Next row (WS)* P to last 2 sts, p2tog.

Next row K2tog, k to last st, M1, k1. Rep last 2 rows once more—11 sts.

Next row P to last 2 sts, p2tog.

Next row K2tog, k to end. Rep last 2 rows once more. Bind off rem 7 sts.

Right front leg With WS facing, join yarn to 13 sts on opposite side and work as foll:

Next row (WS) P2tog, p to end.

Next row K1, M1, k to last 2 sts, k2tog. Rep last 2 rows once more—11 sts.

Next row P2tog, p to end.

Next row K to last 2 sts, k2tog. Rep last 2 rows once more. Bind off rem 7 sts.

Left back leg Place 9 sts from holder onto needle, ready to work a RS row. Work as foll:

Next row (RS) Join MC and bind off 1 st, k to end. Work rem 8 sts as for right back leg.

GUSSET AND LOWER BODY

With larger needles and MC, cast on 3 sts. Work 2 rows in St st.

Inc row (RS) K1, M1, k to last st, M1, k1. Work 3 rows even. Rep last 4 rows 4 times more—13 sts. Work 4 more rows even in St st. Place markers each side of row. Shape back legs.

Inc row (RS) K1, M1, k to last st, M1, k1. Work 1 row even. Rep last 2 rows 5 times more—25 sts.

Left back leg *Next row (RS)* K8, place rem 17 sts on a holder. Work these 8 sts as for right back leg of upper body.

Center of body Place 17 sts from holder onto needle, ready to work a RS row. Join MC and work as foll:

Next row (RS) K9, place rem 8 sts on a holder. Work 7 more rows in St st on 9 sts.

Shape front legs *Row 1 (RS)* K1, M1, k3, M1, k1, M1, k3, M1, k1—13 sts.

Row 2 and all WS rows Purl.

Row 3 K1, M1, k5, M1, k1, M1, k5, M1, k1—17 sts.

Row 5 K1, M1, k7, M1, k1, M1, k7, M1, k1—21 sts.

Row 7 K1, M1, k9, M1, k1, M1, k9, M1, k1—25 sts.

Rows 9 and 11 K1, M1, k to last st, M1, k1—29 sts.

Row 12 Purl.

Next row (RS) K1, M1, k11, bind off center 5 sts, k to last st, M1, k1. Cont on last 13 sts only.

Right front leg *Next row (WS)* P to last 2 sts, p2tog.

Next row K2tog, k to last st, M1, k1. Rep last 2 rows once more—11 sts.

Next row P to last 2 sts, p2tog.

Next row K2tog, k to end. Rep last 2 rows once more. Bind off rem 7 sts.

Left front leg With WS facing, join yarn to 13 sts on opposite side and work as foll:

Next row (WS) P2tog, p to end.

Next row K1, M1, k to last 2 sts, k2tog. Rep last 2 rows once more—11 sts.

Next row P2tog, p to end.

Next row K to last 2 sts, k2tog. Rep last 2 rows once more. Bind off rem 7 sts.

Right back leg With RS facing, join MC and work rem 8 sts as for right back leg of upper body.

HEAD

With larger needles and MC, cast on 7 sts. P 1 row on WS.

Next row (RS) K1, [M1, k1] 6 times—13 sts. Work 1 row even.

Next row K1, [M1, k1] 12 times—25 sts. Work 3 rows even.

Next row K2, [M1, k3] 7 times, M1, k2—33 sts. Work 13 rows even.

Shape nose *Next row (RS)* K1, [k2tog] 16 times—17 sts.

Work 5 rows even.

Next row (RS) K1, [k2tog] 8 times—9 sts. Break yarn, leaving a long end. Draw yarn through sts, pull tog tightly and fasten off. Sew seam leaving an opening at back to insert stuffing.

OUTER EARS (MAKE 2)

With larger needles and MC, cast on 3 sts.

Row 1 (WS) K3.

Row 2 [K1, M1] twice, k1.

Row 3 K5.

Row 4 K1, M1, k3, M1, k1.

Rows 5-7 K7.

Row 8 K1, M1, k5, M1, k1.

Rows 9-23 K9.

Row 24 K1, ssk, k to last 3 sts, k2tog, k1.

Row 25 Knit.

Rows 26 and 27 Rep rows 24 and 25.

Row 28 K5.

Row 29 K1, SK2P, k1—3 sts.

Row 30 SK2P. Fasten off.

INNER EARS (MAKE 2)

With smaller needles and A, cast on 4 sts. Work 30 rows of Chart. Bind off rem 4 sts.

TAIL

With larger needles and MC, cast on 7 sts. Work 8 rows in St st. Bind off, leaving a long end. Thread end onto yarn needle and draw around outer edge of tail, gathering up to form round shape and leaving an opening to insert stuffing.

FINISHING

With WS tog, sew inner ear to outer ear. Sew lower body to upper body, matching markers at back. Leave an opening at neck and back to insert stuffing. Stuff head and body firmly. Sew openings closed. Sew head to neck. Stuff tail. Sew to body. Pleat bottom edges of ears and sew to head. Embroider face and paw details, using photo as a guide.

Inner Ear Chart

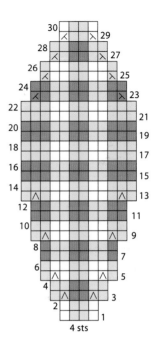

4 sts

Color Key

☐ White (A)

▨ Powder Blue (B)

▨ Sky Blue (C)

Stitch Key

⊠ SKP on RS

⊡ K 2 tog on RS

△ Make 1 (M1)

Hop hither and yon with this portable pal, striped and dotted in true emerald and olive tones. Curly crocheted webbed feet give his gangly limbs a fanciful flourish and complement his dapper bow tie and quaint button eyes. Who said it ain't easy being green?

leapin' lizard

Designed by Amy Bahrt

materials

Cotton Classic II by Tahki Yarns/
Tahki•Stacy Charles, Inc., 1¾oz/50g
balls, each approx 74yds/68m (cotton)
1 skein each in #2726 Citrus Green (A)
and #2764 Kelly Green (B)
Small amount of #2997 Red (C)
for embroidering mouth
One pair size 7 (4.5mm) needles
OR SIZE TO OBTAIN GAUGE
Fiberfill
Yarn needle
Size G/6 (4.5mm) crochet hook
2 White ½"/13mm buttons for eyes

FINISHED MEASUREMENTS

10"/25.5cm long

GAUGE

18 sts and 24 rows to 4"/10cm over St st using size 7 (4.5mm) needles.
TAKE TIME TO CHECK YOUR GAUGE.

NOTE

When working spots on frog's body, use a separate length of B for each spot. When changing colors, twist yarns on WS to prevent holes in the work. Or, if desired, the spots can be worked later with duplicate stitch.

BACK

With A, cast on 10 sts. Work 34 rows of Body Chart. Work chart row 35 as foll: Ssk, k2, join 2nd length of A and bind off 2 sts, k 1 more st, k2tog. Bind off all sts.

FRONT

Work as for back through row 25 of chart. Bind off 10 sts.

FACE

With A, cast on 8 sts. Work 10 rows of Face Chart. Work last row of chart as for last row of back.

Continued on page 30

leapin' lizard

Continued from page 28

ARMS (MAKE 2)

With A, cast on 7 sts. Work in St st as foll: [work 2 rows with A, 2 rows with B] 5 times, end 2 rows A. Bind off. Sew side and top seam.

LEGS (MAKE 2)

Work as for arms, working instructions in brackets 6 times.

FINISHING

Sew front and back of body tog, leaving opening at top. Stuff firmly. Sew on face, leaving opening at bottom. Stuff. Pull lower edge of face down slightly over top edge of body front and stitch closed. Sew arms onto upper body.

WEBBING

With crochet hook and B, join yarn with sl st to end of each arm, *ch 7, join with sl st in next st; rep from * twice more. Fasten off. Sew legs onto lower body and work webbing as for arms. With B, sew buttons on face for eyes. With B, embroider nostrils on face. With yarn needle and C, embroider chain st under purl ridge on face for mouth.

TIE

With crochet hook and B, work 17"/43cm chain and fasten off. Tie bow around neck.

Face Chart

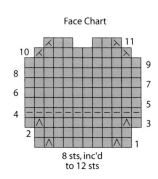

8 sts, inc'd
to 12 sts

Body Chart

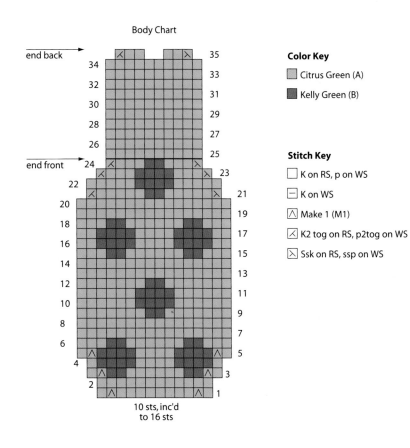

end back

end front

10 sts, inc'd
to 16 sts

Color Key

◻ Citrus Green (A)

◼ Kelly Green (B)

Stitch Key

◻ K on RS, p on WS

⊟ K on WS

△ Make 1 (M1)

◁ K2 tog on RS, p2tog on WS

▷ Ssk on RS, ssp on WS

Go for bold with this vibrant patchwork cub that showcases an array of decorative stitching. If you've always been intimidated by Intarsia colorwork, this accessible introduction will turn you into a master in no time.

rainbow brights

materials

Encore DK by Plymouth Yarns
1½oz/50g each approx 150yds/
138m (acrylic/wool)
1 ball each #133 Royal Blue (A);
#1383 Orange (B);
#54 Green (C); #1384 Purple (D);
#1385 Pink (E); #1382 Yellow (G);
Country 8-ply by Cleckheaton/
Plymouth Yarns, 1½oz/50g each
approx 105yds/94m (wool)
1 ball each #2250 Lime (F);
#2230 Turquoise (H); #1386 Red (I)
One pair size 8 (5mm) needles
Small amount of black yarn
for embroidery
One pair size 5 (3.75mm) needles
OR SIZE TO OBTAIN GAUGE
Stitch holder
Fiberfill
Yarn needle

Designed by Cleckheaton Design Studio

FINISHED MEASUREMENTS

Size approx 14"/35.5cm tall

GAUGE

24 sts and 34 rows to 4"/10cm in St st using size 8 (5mm) needles.

TAKE TIME TO CHECK YOUR GAUGE.

STITCH GLOSSARY

2-st dec row Work across to 2 sts before marker, dec, slip marker, dec, work across.

4-st dec row Dec at beg of row, work across to 2 sts before marker, dec, slip marker, dec, work across to last 2 sts, dec.

2-st inc row Work across and inc in st right before and right after marker.

4-st inc row Inc at beg of row, work across and inc in st right before and right after marker, work across and inc in last st.

NOTES

Bear is worked in St st. Color is worked using the Intarsia method: use a separate skein of yarn for each color area. When changing colors in middle of row at marker, drop old color to WS and pick up new color from underneath. This will twist both yarns tog to avoid a hole. Decorate finished teddy with embroidery stitches, see page 125.

Continued on page 34

rainbow brights

Continued from page 32

BACK

Cast on 2 sts with B, place marker (pm), then cast on 2 sts with A—4 sts. Working in colors as established, inc in each st across—8 sts. Work 2-st Inc Row on next row—10 sts. Work 4-st Inc Row on next row—14 sts. Work 2-st Inc Row on next 3 rows—20 sts. Work 4-st Inc Row on next row—24 sts. P next row.

Next Row *Work 2-st Inc Row, p next row—26 sts. Work 4-st Inc Row, p next row—30 sts. Rep from * until there are 42 sts, end with WS row. Work 2 rows even.

Next Row Work 4-st Inc Row—46 sts.

Next Row (WS) Work in St st, inc 1 st at each end of every 4th row twice—50 sts. Then work 5 rows even in St st. Change colors

Next Row (RS) K25 C, k 25 D. Working in colors as established, dec 1 st each end of every 4th row 4 times, end with a RS row—42 sts.

Next Row (WS) Work 2-st Dec Row on next 3 rows—36 sts. Work 4-st Dec Row on next row—32 sts. Work 2-st Dec Row on next 3 rows—26 sts. Work 4-st Dec Row on next 2 rows. Bind off rem 18 sts.

Front Cast on as for back. K2 A, k2 B. Working in colors as established. P 1 row, then inc in each st across on next row—8 sts.

Next Row *Work 2-st Inc Row, p next row. Work 4-st Inc Row, p next row. Rep from * until there are 50 sts. Work 2 rows even, inc 1 st each end of next row, work 1 row even. Change colors.

Next Row (RS) K26 C, k26 D. Working in colors as established, work 5 rows even in St st.

Next Row [Work 4-st Dec Row, then work 3 rows even] 3 times—40 sts.

Next Row (RS) [Work 4-st Dec Row, p next row. Work 2-st Dec Row, p next row] twice—28 sts. Work 4-st Dec Row on next 2 rows, bind off rem 20 sts.

HEAD

With E, cast on 18 sts for left side, pm, with F cast on 18 sts for right side. Working in colors as established, work 2 rows in St st.

Row 3 (RS) K across, inc in first and last st—20 sts.

Rows 4 and 6 Purl across.

Row 5 Work 4-st Inc Row—42 sts.

Row 7 Work 2-st Inc Row—44 sts.

Row 8 (WS) Purl to 2 sts before marker, inc in both sts, sl marker, inc in next 2 sts, p to end—48 sts.

Row 9 Knit.

Row 10 Rep row 8—52 sts. Rep rows 7–10 twice more, then work row 7 again—74 sts. Work 1 row even. Work left and right sides separately. (Gusset piece will fit into this area—see photo.)

Left Side of Head K to marker, turn, place sts for right side of head on holder. Bind off 2 sts at beg of next row—35 sts. Dec 1 st at end of next 4 RS rows—31 sts. Purl, then dec 1 st at each end of next 2 RS rows, then every row until there are 9 sts. Bind off rem sts.

Right Side of Head Sl sts from holder onto needle, ready to beg RS row. Cont with F, bind off 2 sts at beg of row—35 sts. Dec 1 st at beg of next 4 RS rows—31 sts. Purl, then dec 1 st at each end of next 2 RS rows, then every row until there are 9 sts. Bind off rem sts.

Head Gusset

Cast on 7 sts with G. Work in St st and inc 1 st each end of 5th row, and then every 6th row until there are 21 sts. Work 5 rows even, then dec 1 st each end of next row, and then every

4th row until 7 sts rem, then every other row twice—3 sts. Work 1 row even, then k1, k2tog, turn. P2 tog, fasten off.

EARS (MAKE 2)

Cast on 18 sts with A and work 8 rows in St st. Dec 1 st at each end of next 3 RS rows—12 sts, then every row 3 times—6 sts. Work 1 row even, break off A. Change to H, work 1 row even, then inc 1 st at each end of every row 3 times—12 sts, then next 3 RS rows—18 sts. Work 7 rows even. Bind off rem 7 sts. Work other ear the same using I and D.

ARMS (MAKE 2)

Cast on 2 sts with E, pm, cast on 2 sts with H. Working in colors as established, inc in each st across—8 sts.

Next Row [Work 2-st Inc Row, then 4-st Inc Row] 3 times—26 sts. Then work 2-st Inc Row on next 3 RS rows—32 sts. P next row.

Next Row (RS) [Inc in first st, work rest of row as 2-st Dec Row and inc in last st. P next row] 5 times—32 sts. Work 6 rows even.

Next Row [Work 2-st Inc Row, then work 3 rows even] twice—36 sts. Change colors.

Next Row (RS) With G (in place of H) and F (in place of E), [k2 tog, work rest of row as 2-st Inc Row and dec at end of row. Work 3 rows even] 6 times—36 sts. Work 1 row even. Then work 4-st Dec Row 5 times. Bind off rem 8 sts.

LEGS (MAKE 2)

Cast on 26 sts with C, pm, cast on 26 sts with B. Working in colors as established, work 2 rows in St st. Work 2-st Dec Row every row until 42 sts rem, work 1 row even. Work 2-st Dec Row on next 2 RS rows—38 sts, then every 4 rows twice—34 sts. Work 5 rows even, then work 4-st Inc Row—38 sts. Work 1 row even. Change colors: With A (in place of C) and I (in place of B), work 6 rows even, then work 4-st Inc Row—42 sts. Work 7 rows even, then work 4-st Inc sts Row—46 sts. Work 5 rows even, then work 4-st Dec Row—42 sts. Work 3 rows even, then work 4-st Dec Row, then every RS row twice—30 sts, then every row 5 times. Bind off rem 10 sts.

Sole (make 2) Beg at Toe, cast on 4 sts with G, work 2 rows. Cast on 2 sts at beg of next 2 rows—8 sts. Then inc 1 st at each end of next 2 rows—12 sts. Work even for 14 rows. Dec 1 st at each end of next 2 RS rows, then every row 3 times—2 sts. K2tog, fasten off.

Assembly Sew arm seams, leaving end open to stuff. Sew leg seams leaving bottom of foot open. Stuff, and then sew on sole. Sew gusset to right and left sides of head: cast-on edge of gusset goes where right and left sides separate at the nose. Sew back head seam leaving neck open for stuffing. Sew front and back body pieces tog, leaving open at bound-off edges for neck. Firmly stuff the head, body, and arms. Finish sewing arms shut. Sew head to body at neck. Fold ears in half and sew tog at side edges; sew to sides of head. Arms and legs can be sewn individually onto body, or by stitching each pair tog through body so that arms and legs move. Using black yarn, embroider face as shown in picture. Using lazy daisy, blanket stitch, feather stitch, and straight stitch, embroider Teddy using photo as a guide.

This slouch of a bunny has the sweetly melancholy attributes of an antique rag doll. He's floppy and funny and utterly fetching in a combination of heather gray garter and stockinette stitches, but it's the snazzy overalls that really give him character.

silly rabbit

materials for bunny
Bebé Lang by Lang/Berroco, Inc.,
1¾oz/50g balls, each
approx 219yds/203m 100% wool
1 ball each in #0002 Ecru (A)
and #0070 Grey (B)
One pair size 8 (5mm) needles
OR SIZE TO OBTAIN GAUGE
Small amount of black yarn
for eyes and nose
Stitch holders and fiberfill
Yarn needle

materials for overalls
Omega by Lang/Berroco, Inc.,
1¾oz/50g balls, each approx
108yds/100m (cotton)
1 ball each in #2932 Blue (MC)
and #2903 White (CC)
One pair size 6 (4mm) needles
OR SIZE TO OBTAIN GAUGE
Two buttons
Yarn needle

FINISHED MEASUREMENTS

14"/35.6cm tall

GAUGES

Bunny 20 sts and 28 rows to 4"/10cm over St st using size 8 (5mm) needles and 1 strand each A and B held tog.

Overalls 21 sts and 26 rows to 4"/10cm over St st using size 6 (4mm) needles.

TAKE TIME TO CHECK YOUR GAUGES.

NOTE

Work with 1 strand each of A and B held tog throughout.

HEAD

Side Cast on 13 sts. K 2 rows.

Row 3 (WS) Purl. Cont in St st as foll:

Row 4 Inc 1 st in first st, k to end. Work 3 rows even. Rep last 4 rows twice more—16 sts.

Row 16 (RS) Bind off 3 sts, k to end. Work 1 row even.

Row 18 Bind off 2 sts, k to last 2 sts, dec 1 st. Work 1 row even. Rep last 2 rows once more.

Row 22 Bind off 2 sts, k to end. Work 1 row even. Bind off rem 5 sts. Work 2nd side to correspond, reversing shaping.

Continued on page 38

silly rabbit

Continued from page 37

Center Cast on 10 sts. K 2 rows. Beg with a p row, cont in St st for 25 rows.

Row 28 Dec 1 st each side. Work 5 rows even. Rep last 6 rows twice more. Bind off rem 4 sts. Sew sides of head to center of head and stuff. Embroider eyes and nose foll photo.

EARS (MAKE 2)

Cast on 16 sts. Work in garter st for 13 rows. Dec 1 st each side on next row. Work 5 rows even. Dec 1 st each side on next row. Work 3 rows even. Rep last 10 rows twice more. Bind off rem 4 sts. Sew to top of head foll photo for placement.

ARMS (MAKE 2)

Cast on 6 sts and work in St st, inc 1 st each side every other row 7 times—20 sts. Work even until there are 30 rows from beg. Dec 1 st each side on next row, then every 3rd row 3 times more. Bind off rem 12 sts. Sew seams and stuff.

BODY BACK

Cast on 28 sts. Beg with a p row and work in St st for 19 rows.

Next row (RS) Work 14 sts, join 2nd ball of yarn and work to end. Cont to work both sides at once with separate balls of yarn, work 1 row even.

Dec row 1 (RS) Dec 1 st, work to end of first half; on 2nd half, work to last 2 sts, dec 1 st. Work 3 rows even. [*Dec row 2* Dec 1 st, work to last 2 sts of first side, dec 1 st; on 2nd side dec 1 st each side. Work 3 rows even] 3 times. Bind off rem 7 sts each side.

LEGS (MAKE 2)

Cast on 13 sts and work in St st for 42 rows. Place sts on a holder. Work a 2nd leg in same way. Join both legs and work even on 26 sts for 2 rows. Dec 1 st each side on next row. Work 3 rows even. [Dec 1 st each side of next row. Work 1 row even] 5 times. Work 4 rows even. Bind off rem 14 sts. Sew cast-on edge of back to bound-off edge of legs, foll diagram. Sew center seam of back.

BODY FRONT

Cast on 13 sts for one leg and work in St st for 42 rows. Place sts on a holder. Work a 2nd leg in same way. Join both legs and work even all 26 sts for 20 rows.

Next row (RS) Work 13 sts, join 2nd ball of yarn and work to end. Working both sides at once with separate balls, work 3 rows even. Work dec row 2 as for back. Work 3 rows even. Work dec row 1 as for back. Work 1 row even. Work dec row 1. Work 3 rows even. Work dec row 2. Work 3 rows even. Work dec row 1. Work 1 row even. Bind off rem 6 sts each side. Sew center seam.

FINISHING

Sew front to back and stuff. Sew on head. Sew on arms. For foot, work a running st around leg 1"/2.5cm above bottom of leg.

OVERALLS

With MC, cast on 48 sts for top side of leg and k 2 rows. Cont in St st for 10 rows. Bind off 2 sts at beg of next 2 rows. Dec 1 st each side every other row 4 times. Work even until piece measures 5"/13cm from beg. Dec 1 st each side every other row twice. Work 4 rows in garter st. Bind off. Work back side of leg in same way. Make a 2nd leg in same way.

STRAPS (MAKE 2)

With MC, cast on 3 sts and work in garter st for 7"/18cm. Bind off.

FINISHING

Block pieces. With CC, whip st vertical stripes evenly spaced on pants foll photo. Sew front and back seams. Sew crotch seam. Sew straps and buttons to overalls.

Diagram

This downy duckling is ideally proportioned for small fingers just learning to hold and grab. Stitching with two strands of soothing, silky eyelash yarn makes this tiny guy especially voluminous and cuddly.

b i r d   i n   h a n d

materials
Fun Fur by Lion Brand Yarns,
1³⁄₄oz/50g balls, each approx
60yds/54m (polyester)
1 skein in #100 White (MC)
2 skeins Orange embroidery floss (A)
1 skein Black embroidery floss (B)
One pair size 7 (4.5mm) needles
OR SIZE TO OBTAIN GAUGE
Fiberfill
Yarn needle
2 double-pointed needles (dpn)

Designed by Barbara Boulton

FINISHED MEASUREMENTS

6½"/16.5cm long

GAUGE

26 sts and 40 rows to 4"/10cm over Pat st with Fun Fur using size 7 (4.5mm) needles.
TAKE TIME TO CHECK YOUR GAUGE.

NOTE

Sl sts purlwise wyif.

BILL

With 2 strands of A held tog, cast on 8 sts.

Rows 1-12 *K1, sl 1; rep from * to end.

Next row Sl first st onto dpn, sl next st onto 2nd dpn. Cont alternately slipping sts first onto one dpn, then onto 2nd dpn, until there are 4 sts on each dpn. Cut yarn, leaving a 10"/25.5cm long tail. Thread tail onto yarn needle and run through sts on first dpn (sts 1, 3, 5 and 7), then through sts on 2nd dpn (sts 8, 6, 4, 2). Set aside.

BODY

With MC, cast on 24 sts.

Row 1 *K1, sl 1; rep from * to end.

Rows 2-13 Cast on 2 sts, then *k1, sl 1; rep from * to end. After row 13, there are 48 sts.

Rows 14-35 Rep row 1.

Row 36 Bind off 6 sts (1 st rem on RH needle), sl 1, *k1, sl 1; rep from * to end—42 sts.

Row 37 Bind off 18 sts, sl 1, *k1, sl 1; rep from * to end—24 sts.

Rows 38-55 Rep row 1.

Rows 56-61 Bind off 2 sts, sl 1, *k1, sl 1; rep from * to end. After row 61, there are 12 sts. Place alternate sts onto dpns as before—6 sts on each dpn. Cut yarn, leaving a 12"/30.5cm long tail. Run yarn through sts as before. Loosen and open the top of the knitting. Gently stuff body and head with fiberfill. Draw up the thread to close the top of the head. Draw yarn needle down through head to the neck. Wrap yarn a couple of times around neck to define it. Make a couple of small sts to secure the end and secure yarn to inside. With B doubled, make 3 or 4 small sts on each side of head for eyes.

Sew bill to lower front of head. Make 6-8 sts to hold it firmly and secure yarn end to inside.

WINGS (MAKE 2)

With MC, cast on 10 sts. K 8 rows.

Next row K2tog, k to end.

Next row Knit. Rep last 2 rows 6 times more—3 sts.

Next row K3tog. Fasten off. Cut yarn, leaving a 6"/15cm long tail. With shaped edge of wing parallel to body, secure one corner of cast-on edge to body, just under head. Tie 6"/15cm tails of both wings tog and secure ends to inside of back end of body.

LEGS (MAKE 2)

Cut six 18"/46cm lengths of A. Thread ends onto yarn needle and run floss through 3 sts on side of body. Adjust all 12 ends until they are equal length. Divide ends into 3 groups of 4 and braid. Tie a knot approx 1"/2.5cm from end. Trim ends.

With a cozy blue pullover and plenty of fur, this blond grizzly is ready to either hunker down for the winter or take to the slopes! His shaggy wool blend nap and toddler-size body make him extra huggable, and his snowflake sweater makes him super stylish.

h i - b e a r - n a t i o n

materials for bear
Yogi by Filatura Di Crosa/Tahki•Stacy
Charles, Inc., 1³⁄₄oz/50g balls,
each approx 55yds/50m
(wool/acrylic/polyamide)
6 balls in #57 Lt Brown
Small amount of Brown
for embroidery
One pair size 10 (6mm) needles
OR SIZE TO OBTAIN GAUGE
Stitch holders
Fiberfill
Yarn needle

materials for bear's sweater
501 by Filatura Di Crosa/Tahki•Stacy
Charles, Inc., 1³⁄₄oz/50g balls,
each approx 136yds/125m (wool)
3 balls in #2116 Turquoise
Small piece of White felt
Fabric glue
One pair size 7 (4.5mm) needles
OR SIZE TO OBTAIN GAUGE
Size E/4 (3.5mm) crochet hook
Yarn needle

Designed by Veronica Manno

BEAR

FINISHED MEASUREMENTS

Height (from top of head to tip of paws) 24"/61cm

Width around body 21"/53.5cm

GAUGE

8½ sts and 16 rows to 4"/10cm over St st using size 10 (6mm) needles.

TAKE TIME TO CHECK YOUR GAUGE.

HEAD

Side Cast on 12 sts. K 2 rows, p 1 row on WS. Cont in St st, inc 1 st at beg of next row (side edge) and cont to inc 1 st at side edge every other row twice more—15 sts. Work even until piece measures 3½"/9cm from beg.

Next row (RS) Bind off 7 sts, work to end. Work 1 row even. Dec 1 st each side on next row. Work 1 row even.

Next row Dec 1 st, work to end. Work 1 row even. Rep last 2 rows once more. Bind off rem 4 sts. Work 2nd side to correspond, reversing shaping.

Back Cast on 12 sts and k 2 rows. P 1 row on WS.

Next row (RS) [K3, inc 1 st in next st] twice, k to end—14 sts. Work 3 rows even.

Next row [K4, inc 1 st in next st] twice, k to end—16 sts. Work 5 rows even. Dec 1 st each side on next row, then every other row twice more—10 sts. Bind off 2 sts at beg of next 2 rows. Bind off rem 6 sts.

Continued on page 44

h i - b e a r - n a t i o n

Continued from page 42

Center Cast on 4 sts. Work in St st, inc 1 st each side on rows 5, 11, 15 and 17. Work even until there are 22 rows from beg. Bind off rem 12 sts.

Base of nose/chin Cast on 2 sts and work in St st, inc 1 st each side every other row 4 times—10 sts. Bind off 3 sts at beg of next 2 rows. Bind off rem 4 sts. Sew sides of head to back head. Sew base of nose/chin to center piece. Sew center piece between side pieces. Stuff head and embroider nose, eyes and mouth (see photo).

EARS (MAKE 2)

Cast on 10 sts and work in St st for 4 rows. Dec 1 st each side on next row, then every other row once more. Inc 1 st each side on next RS row then every other row once more. Work 3 rows even. Bind off rem 10 sts. With WS tog, fold in half and sew. Sew to top of head foll photo.

BODY BACK

Cast on 26 sts for underside and work in St st for 17 rows.

Next row (WS) Work 13 sts, join 2nd ball of yarn and work to end. Working both sides at once with separate balls, work 1 row even.

Dec row 1 (WS) P2tog, work to end of first half; on 2nd half work to last 2 sts, p2tog. Work 3 rows even.

Dec row 2 P2tog, work to last 2 sts of first half, p2tog; work 2nd half as for first half. Work 1 row even. Rep dec row 1. Work 3 rows even. Work dec row 2. Work 1 row even. Work dec row 1. Work 1 row even. Bind off rem 6 sts each side.

Bottom leg Cast on 6 sts and work in St st, inc 1 st each side every other row once, every 4th row twice—12 sts. Work even until piece 39 rows have been worked from beg. Place sts on a holder. Make a 2nd piece in same way. Join both pieces and work on 24 sts, dec 1 st each side every other row 5 times. Bind off rem 14 sts. Sew center seam of body back. Sew cast-on edge of body back to bound-off of back legs, foll diagram 1.

ARMS (MAKE 2)

Cast on 5 sts for shoulder edge and work in St st for 1 row. Cast on 2 sts at beg of next 2 rows. Inc 1 st each side every other row 5 times—19 sts. Work 13 rows even. Dec 1 st each side every other row 3 times, every 4th row once—11 sts. Work 1 row even. Bind off. Sew seams and stuff.

BODY FRONT

Cast on 6 sts for underside of foot and work in St st for 11 rows. Place sts on a holder. Make a 2nd piece in same way. Join both pieces and work on 12 sts for 30 rows. Place sts on a holder. Make a 2nd piece in same way. Join both pieces on one needle—24 sts. Work even for 18 rows. Divide work in half and work as foll: Work 1 row even. Work dec row 2. Work 3 rows even. Work dec row 1. Work 3 rows even. Work dec row 2. Work 3 rows even. Work dec row 1. Work 1 row even. Bind off rem 6 sts each side. Sew center seam. Sew foot foll diagram 2.

FINISHING

Sew body front to back and stuff. Sew on head. Sew on arms.

BEAR SWEATER

FINISHED MEASUREMENTS

Chest 24"/61cm

Length 10"/25.5cm

Upper arm 12"/30.5cm

GAUGE

20 sts and 28 rows to 4"/10cm over St st using size 7 (4.5mm) needles.

TAKE TIME TO CHECK YOUR GAUGE.

BACK

Cast on 60 sts and work in k2, p2 rib for 6 rows.

Work in St st until piece measures 10"/25.5cm from beg. Bind off all sts.

FRONT

Work same as back until piece measures 8½"/21.5cm from beg.

Neck shaping *Next row (RS)* K15, join 2nd ball of yarn and bind off center 30 sts, work to end. Work both sides at once until same length as back. Bind off all sts.

SLEEVES

Cast on 50 sts and work in k2, p2 rib for 6 rows. Work in St st, inc 1 st each side every 4th row 5 times—60 sts. Work even until piece measures 5"/12.5cm from beg. Bind off.

FINISHING

Sew shoulder seams. Place markers 6"/15.5cm down from shoulders on front and back. Sew top of sleeve to front and back between markers. Sew side and sleeve seams. With RS facing and crochet hook work 1 rnd sc evenly around neck edge. Cut out snowflake from white felt and glue in center of front (see photo).

Snowflake Template

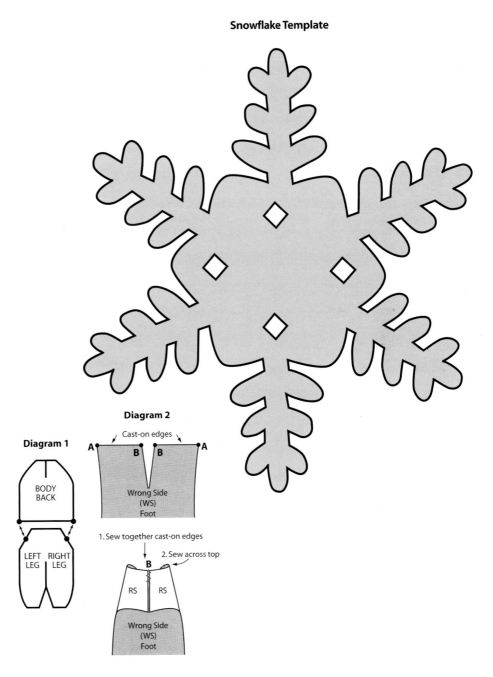

Diagram 1

BODY BACK

LEFT LEG   RIGHT LEG

Diagram 2

Cast-on edges

A   B   B   A

Wrong Side (WS) Foot

1. Sew together cast-on edges

2. Sew across top

B

RS   RS

Wrong Side (WS) Foot

This sassy striped circus character is so much fun to make.
Simply string multicolored crocheted discs together on elastic for flexible arms and legs.
Attach a jaunty cap for more personality.

send in the clown

Designed by Sandi Prosser

materials

Astra by Patons®, 1¾oz/50g balls,
each approx 133yds/122m (acrylic)
1 ball each in #2740 Purple (A),
#2911 Spring Green (B),
#2225 Crayon Red (C),
#8742 Ultra Blue (D),
#2941 School Bus Yellow (E)
and #8728 Hot Fuchsia (F)
Size H/8 (5mm) crochet hook
OR SIZE TO OBTAIN GAUGE
Fiberfill
Black embroidery floss
1 yd/1m of elastic cord
Four ⅝"/15mm yellow buttons
Yarn needle

FINISHED MEASUREMENTS

Approx 9½"/24cm long

GAUGE

One circle to 2½"/6.5cm using size H/8 (5mm) hook.
TAKE TIME TO CHECK YOUR GAUGE.

NOTE

To dec 1 sc, [insert hook into next st and draw up a lp] twice, yo and draw through all 3 lps on hook.

CIRCLES

Make 11 using A and 10 each using B, C, D, E, and F. Ch 6. Join ch with a sl st forming a ring.

Rnd 1 Ch 3 (always counts as 1 dc), work 14 dc in ring—15 dc. Join rnd with a sl st in 3rd ch of ch-3.

Rnd 2 Ch 3, dc in same sp as sl st, work 2 dc in each st around—30 dc. Join rnd with a sl st in 3rd ch of ch-3. Fasten off.

HEAD

Beg at top, with E, ch 3. Join ch with a sl st forming a ring.

Rnd 1 Ch 1 (always counts as 1 sc), work 5 dc in ring—6 sc. Join this rnd and all rem rnds with a sl st in ch-1.

Rnd 2 Ch 1, sc in same sp as sl st, work 2 sc in each st around—12 sc.

Rnd 3 Ch 1, sc in same sp as sl st, sc in next st, *work 2 sc in next st, sc in next st; rep from * around—18 sc.

Continued on page 48

s e n d   i n   t h e   c l o w n

Continued from page 46

Rnd 4 Ch 1, sc in same sp as sl st, sc in next 2 sts, *work 2 sc in next st, sc in next 2 sts; rep from * around—24 sc.

Rnd 5 Ch 1, sc in same sp as sl st, sc in next 3 sts, *work 2 sc in next st, sc in next 3 sts; rep from * around—30 sc.

Rnds 6-13 Ch 1, sc in each st around.

Rnd 14 Ch 1, *dec 1 sc over next 2 sts, sc in next 3 sts; rep from * around—24 sc.

Rnd 15 Ch 1, *dec 1 sc over next 2 sts, sc in next 2 sts; rep from * around—18 sc.

Rnd 16 Ch 1, *dec 1 sc over next 2 sts, sc in next st; rep from * around—12 sc. Fasten off.

HAT

Beg at top, with D, ch 3. Join ch with a sl st forming a ring.

Rnd 1 Ch 1 (always counts as 1 sc), work 5 dc in ring—6 sc. Join this rnd and all rem rnds with a sl st in ch-1.

Rnd 2 Ch 1, sc in each st around.

Rnds 3-6 Rep rnds 2-5 as for head—30 sc.

Rnd 7 Ch 1, sc in each st around. Ch 1, turn.

Brim Rnd 8 Sc in each st around.

Rnds 9 and 10 Ch 1, sc in each st around.

Fasten off.

FINISHING

Stuff head with fiberfill; sew bottom opening closed.

Embroidery Using all six strands of floss in needle, embroider nose, mouth eyes and eyebrows in chain stitch. Using B, sew hat to head at an angle, as shown.

ASSEMBLY

Thread on all circles from RS, making sure to keep elastic cord relaxed. Cut elastic in half. Thread one length into yarn needle, then secure end to bottom of head with a few small back stitches.

Neck Thread on A, B, C and D.

First arm Thread on B, C, D, E, F, A, B, C, D, E, F

and A. From WS of button, insert needle up through one hole, then down through other hole. Insert needle back through all arm and neck circles. Secure to bottom of head with a few small back stitches.

Body Insert needle through neck circles. Thread on E, F, A, B, C, D, E, F and A.

First leg Thread on B, C, D, E, F, A, B, C, D, E, F and A. Thread on button as for first arm. Insert needle back through all leg, body and neck circles. Secure to bottom of head with a few small back stitches; trim off excess elastic.

Second arm Thread remaining length of elastic into tapestry needle, then secure end to bottom of head with a few small back stitches. Insert needle through neck circles. Cont to work as for first arm.

Second leg Insert needle through all neck and body circles. Cont work as for first leg.

A playful loop stitch creates the fluffy fleece of a wee lamb in this whimsical tribute to childhood nursery rhymes. Face, feet and ears are done up in black garter stitch for a fetching creature that doesn't need to go ba-a-a to capture your heart.

feeling sheepish

FINISHED MEASUREMENTS

9"/23cm high and 15"/38cm long

GAUGE

19 sts and 26 rows to 4"/10cm over St st with MC using size 7 (4.5mm) needles. TAKE TIME TO CHECK YOUR GAUGE.

LOOP STITCH

K1, but do not drop old st from LH needle, bring yarn to front between the needles and wind it clockwise around your left thumb, bring yarn to back and k into same st on LH needle, sl st off LH needle; sl 2 sts from RH needle back to LH needle and k them tog through back loops.

LOOP STITCH PATTERN

(over an even number of sts)

Rows 1 and 3 (WS) Knit.

Row 2 K1, *loop st, k1; rep from * to last st, k1.

Row 4 K2, *loop st, k1; rep from * to end. Rep rows 1-4 for loop st pat. (over an odd number of sts)

Rows 1 and 3 (WS) Knit.

Row 2 K1, *loop st, k1; rep from * to end.

materials
Top of the Lamb Worsted by Brown
Sheep Yarn Co., 4oz/113g balls,
each approx 190yds/173m (wool)
3 balls in #470 White (MC)
and 1 ball in #210 Black (CC)
½yd/.5m of ¼"/6mm wide ribbon
One pair size 7 (4.5mm) needles
OR SIZE TO OBTAIN GAUGE
Fiberfill

Continued on page 52

Designed by Sandi Prosser

feeling sheepish

Continued from page 51

Row 4 K2, *loop st, k1; rep from * to last st, k1. Rep rows 1-4 for loop st pat.

UPPER BODY

With MC, cast on 48 sts and mark center of row.

Row 1 (WS) Knit.

Shape back legs *Next row (RS)* Cast on 7 sts, then k2, *loop st, k1; rep from * to last st, k1.

Next row Cast on 7 sts, k to end. Rep last 2 rows once more—76 sts. Beg with row 2, work 10 rows in loop st pat (over an even number of sts). Cont in loop st pat as established, bind off 10 sts at beg of next 2 rows. Dec 1 st each side of next 3 rows—50 sts. Work 45 rows even in pat.

Shape front legs Cast on 6 sts at beg of next 2 rows, then 5 sts at beg of next 2 rows—72 sts. Work 12 rows even. Bind off 5 sts at beg of next 2 rows, then 4 sts at beg of next 2 rows. Dec 1 st each side on next row, then every other row 3 times more—46 sts. Dec 1 st each side of next 6 rows—34 sts. Work 3 rows even. Bind off.

Inner legs and tummy With MC, cast on 5 sts and mark center st.

Row 1 (WS) Knit.

Next row (RS) K1, *loop st, k1; rep from * to end.

Next row K1, M1, k to last st, M1, k1. Rep last 2 rows once more—9 sts. Beg with row 2, work loop st pat (over an odd number of sts), inc 1 st each side on 8th row, then every 6th row twice more—15 sts. Work 8 rows even in pat.

Shape back legs *Next row (RS)* Cast on 7 sts, then k1, *loop st, k1; rep from * to last st, k1.

Next row Cast on 7 sts, k to end. Rep last 2 rows once more—43 sts. Work 1 row even.

Next row (WS) K14, k2tog, k11, ssp, k14. Work 1 row even.

Next row K13, k2tog, k11, ssp, k13. Cont to dec 2 sts every other row (working 1 less k st before first dec and after last dec) twice more—35 sts. Work 1 row even. Bind off 10 sts at beg of next 2 rows. Dec 1 st each side of next 3 rows—9 sts.

Shape front legs *Next row (RS)* Cast on 6 sts, then k2, *loop st, k1; rep from * to last st, k1.

Next row Cast on 6 sts, k to end.

Next row Cast on 5 sts, then k2, *loop st, k1; rep from * to last st, k1.

Next row Cast on 5 sts, k to end—31 sts. Work 12 rows even. Bind off 5 sts at beg of next 2 rows, then 4 sts at beg of next 2 rows—13 sts. Dec 1 st each side on next row, then on foll 6th row once more—9 sts. Work 15 rows even. Bind off.

HEAD

Short row wrapping (wrap and turn - w&t) Wyib, sl next st purlwise. Move yarn between the needles to the front. Sl the same st back to LH needle. Turn work.

With MC, cast on 43 sts.

Beg short row shaping *Next row (RS)* K39, w&t.

Next row K37, w&t.

Next row K35 (ending 2 sts before last wrapped st), w&t.

Next row K33 (ending 2 sts before last wrapped st), w&t.

Next 15 rows K to 2 sts before last wrapped st, w&t.

Next 3 rows K to end of row. Break MC.

Nose *Row 1* With CC, K1, [k2tog] 10 times, k1, [ssk] 10 times, k1—23 sts.

Row 2 and all WS rows Knit.

Row 3 K4, k2tog, k2, k2tog, k3, ssk, k2, ssk, k4—19 sts.

Row 5 K6, k2tog, k3, ssk, k6—17 sts.

Row 7 K3, [k2tog] twice, k3, [ssk] twice, k3—13 sts.

Row 9 K4, k2tog, k1, ssk, k4—11 sts.

Row 11 K1, [k2tog] twice, k1, [ssk] twice, k1—7 sts. Cut yarn, leaving a long tail. Thread yarn through sts and pull tog tightly. Sew nose seam. Sew upper body to inner legs and tummy from neck to bottom of front legs (do not sew across bottom of legs).

FRONT FEET

Open front legs flat. With RS facing and CC, pick up and k16 sts along bottom edge of front leg. K 9 rows.

Next row K1, [ssk] 3 times, k2, [k2tog] 3 times, k1—10 sts.

Next row K1, [k2tog] 4 times, k1—6 sts. Cut yarn, leaving a long tail. Thread yarn through sts and pull tog tightly. Sew seam in foot and cont sewing from front across tummy and down the front of back legs.

BACK FEET

Work as for front feet. Match marked sts. Sew seam in foot and cont sewing to marked sts and down other side to other back foot.

EARS (MAKE 2)

With CC, cast on 4 sts. K 1 row.

Next row Inc 1 st in first st, k1, inc 1 st in next st, k1—6 sts. K 3 rows.

Next row K2tog, k2, ssk—4 sts.

Next row Knit.

Next row K2tog, ssk—2 sts.

Next row K2tog. Fasten off last st.

TAIL

With MC, cast on 16 sts. K 2 rows. Bind off.

FINISHING

Stuff head and body. Sew head to body. Sew ears and tail in position. Tie ribbon around neck as shown in photo.

One look at his snazzy stripes and it's obvious that this isn't your
run of the mill serpent! Seven button-connected segments let him slither into
all sorts of shapes, but it's your choice of letters that really make him unique.

name snake

materials

Wintuk by Caron International,
3½oz/100g balls, each approx
150yds/138m (acrylic)
1 ball each in #3005 Christmas Red (A),
#3261 Orange (B), #3256 Jonquil (C),
#3030 Royal (D), #3251 Holiday Green (E),
#3026 Baby Blue (F), #3001 White (G)
and #3009 Black (H)
One pair size 9 (5.5mm) needles
OR SIZE TO OBTAIN GAUGE
Fiberfill
Six 1¼"/32mm round buttons
(1 each green, yellow,
orange and red; 2 royal)
Size ⅑ (5.5mm) crochet hook
Yarn needle

Designed by Edit Nagy

FINISHED MEASUREMENTS

Each section is 5"/12.5cm wide by 6½"/16.5cm tall

GAUGE

16 sts and 22 rows to 4"/10cm over St st using size 9 (5.5mm) needles.
TAKE TIME TO CHECK YOUR GAUGE.

NOTES

Work body sections in St st. Each section is 40 sts wide and 36 rows tall. Letters
are embroidered using duplicate st and color D after sections are completed.

BODY

Section 1 With C, cast on 40 sts. Work 6 rows C, 6 rows E, 6 rows A, 4 rows B, 6
rows C, 6 rows E, 2 rows B. Bind off.

Section 2 With F, cast on 40 sts. Work 8 rows F, 8 rows B, 6 rows A, 6 rows B, 8
rows F. Bind off.

Section 3 With E, cast on 40 sts. Work 8 rows E, 4 rows G, 2 rows E, 6 rows A, 6
rows G, 2 rows E, 8 rows A. Bind off.

Section 4 With F, cast on 40 sts. [Work 6 rows F, 6 rows C] 3 times. Bind off.

Section 5 With C, cast on 40 sts. Work 4 rows C, 6 rows E, [6 rows A, 4 rows C]
twice, 6 rows E. Bind off.

Continued on page 56

name snake

Continued from page 54

HEAD

With F, cast on 40 sts. Work 14 rows in St st.

Dec row (RS) K8, ssk, k to last 10 sts, k2tog, k8.

Rep Dec row every other row 7 times more— 24 sts. Work 5 rows even. Bind off.

TAIL

With F, cast on 40 sts.

Rows 1 and 3 (RS) Knit.

Row 2 and all WS rows Purl.

Rows 5, 7, 9, 11 and 13 K8, ssk, k to last 10 sts, k2tog, k8.

Rows 15 and 16 with D, rep rows 5 and 6. Break D.

Row 17 With F, rep row 5.

Row 19 K1, ssk, k5, ssk, k6, k2tog, k5, k2tog, k1.

Row 21 K1, [ssk, k4] twice, k2tog, k4, k2tog, k1.

Row 23 K1, ssk, k3, ssk, k2, k2tog, k3, k2tog, k1.

Row 25 K1, ssk, k6, k2tog, k1.

Row 26 Purl. Break F.

Row 27 With D, k1, [ssk] twice, [k2tog] twice, k1.

Row 29 K1, ssk, k2tog, k1.

Row 31 Ssk, k2tog. Bind off rem 2 sts.

TONGUE

With crochet hook and A, make a chain 5"/12.5cm long. Work single crochet to last 5 sts, ch 5 (to make the tongue forked). Fasten off.

EYES

With C, cast on 4 sts. Break C. With D, work 4 rows in St st. Cut yarn, leaving a 3"/7.5cm long tail. Draw yarn through sts. Undo the cast-on row and draw the yarn through those sts as well. Tighten yarn ends and knot them.

FINISHING

With D, embroider 1 letter on each section, centering letter from side-to-side and top-to-bottom. Sew long seam. Fold section so that seam falls at back and letter is centered on front. Sew bottom seam. Stuff section with fiberfill. Sew top seam. Sew button at bottom of each section, using matching yarn. With crochet hook and H, crochet a button loop at top of each section. Sew tail seam and fold so that seam falls at back. Stuff tail with fiberfill and sew top seam. With H, make a button loop centered on the flat edge of tail. Sew head seam. Sew eyes to center of head. Sew tongue at point, beg approx 1"/2.5cm deep inside head. Stuff head with fiberfill and sew top seam. Sew button at top. Push in fabric at each side of "mouth" opening creating the jaw dimples and sew tog the lips' sts.

Win over the budding paleontologist in your life with an adorable caricature of the ancient rhino relative, the Triceratops. Complete with its famous three horns and a few decorative felt spots for contrast, this fierce beast isn't so scary to tame.

modern day
dinosaur

FINISHED MEASUREMENTS

20"/51cm tall

GAUGE

23 sts and 31 rows to 4"/10cm over St st, using size 5 (3.75 mm) needles.

TAKE TIME TO CHECK YOUR GAUGE.

NOTES

When changing colors in the middle of a row, twist the color to be used (on WS) underneath and to the right of the color just used. Use separate ball of yarn for each color. When binding off, the last st on RH needle is the first st of the stitch count that directly follows.

LEFT LEG

Sole ** With MC, cast on 5 sts.

Row 1 (RS) Knit. Work in garter st, inc 1 st each side of every row 3 times, then every other row 3 times—17 sts. Work even until piece measures 4"/10cm from beg, end with a WS row. Change to B, work in St st, AT SAME TIME, dec 1 st each side on 3rd row, then every other row 3 times, then every row once. Bind off rem 7 sts.

Top of foot Cast on 80 sts as foll: 26 sts MC, 28 sts B, 26 sts MC. K 1 row and p 1 row matching colors.

Continued on page 60

Shape toes *Row 3* K26 MC, *k8 B, k2 MC; rep from * twice more, k24 MC.

Row 4 P26 MC, *(p2tog, p4, p2tog tbl) B, p2 MC; rep from * twice more, p24 MC—74 sts.

Row 5 (K25, M1, k1) MC, *k6 B, (k1, M1, k1) MC; rep from * twice more, k24 MC—78 sts.

Row 6 P27 MC, *(p2tog, p2, p2tog tbl) B, p3 MC; rep from * twice more, p24 MC—72 sts.

Row 7 (K25, [M1, k1] twice) MC, (SKP, k2tog) B, (k1, M1, k2) MC, (SKP, k2tog) B, (k2, M1, k1) MC, (SKP, k2tog) B, ([k1, M1] twice, k25) MC—72 sts. Break B. With MC, work 5 rows St st.

Shape ankle *Next row (RS)* K21, [k3tog] 10 times, k21—52 sts.** Work 16 rows even.

Next row Bind off 26 sts, p to end—26 sts.

Shape thigh and tail opening *Row 1 (RS)* Bind off 3 sts, k2, [M1, k6] 3 times, k3—26 sts.

Row 2 and all WS rows Purl.

Row 3 Bind off 2 sts, k8, M1, k7, M1, k6, M1, k3—27 sts.

Row 5 Bind off 2 sts, k7, M1, k8, M1, k7, M1, k3—28 sts.

Row 7 Bind off 2 sts, k6, M1, k9, M1, k11—28 sts. Work 7 rows even. Work 3 more rows St st, AT SAME TIME, cast on 2 sts at beg of each RS row—32 sts.

Next row (WS) Bind off 6 sts, p to end—26 sts.

Next row Cast on 2 sts, k to end—28 sts.

Next row Bind off 6 sts, p to end—22 sts.

Next row Cast on 3 sts, k to end—25 sts. Cont in St st, bind off 6 sts at beg of every WS row 3 times. Work 1 row even. Bind off rem 7 sts.

Work as for left leg from ** to **. Work 17 rows even.

Shape thigh and tail opening *Row 1* Bind off 26 sts, k9, (M1, K6) twice, M1, k5—29 sts.

Row 2 Bind off 3 sts, p to end—26 sts.

Row 3 K3, M1, k6, M1, k7, M1, k10—29 sts.

Row 4 Bind off 2 sts, p to end—27 sts.

Row 5 K3, M1, k7, M1, k8, M1, k9—30 sts.

Row 6 Rep row 4—28 sts.

Row 7 K11, M1, k9, M1, k8—30 sts.

Row 8 Rep row 4—28 sts. Work 5 rows even.

Work 3 more rows St st, AT SAME TIME, cast on 2 sts at beg of every WS row twice—32 sts.

Next row (RS) Bind off 6 sts, k to end—26 sts.

Next row Cast on 2 sts, p to end—28 sts.

Next row Bind off 6 sts, k to end—22 sts.

Next row Cast on 3 sts, p to end—25 sts. Cont in St st, bind off 6 sts at beg of every RS row 3 times. Work 1 row even. Bind off rem 7 sts.

With MC, cast on 12 sts. Work 6 rows St st.

Next row K3, M1, k1, M1, k4, M1, k1, M1, k3—16 sts. Work 3 rows even.

Next row K4, M1, k1, M1, k6, M1, k1, M1, k4—20 sts. Work 3 rows even.

Next row K5, M1, k1, M1, k8, M1, k1, M1, k5—24 sts. Work 3 rows even.

Next row K6, M1, k1, M1, k10, M1, k1, M1, k6—28 sts. Work 3 rows even. Cont in St st, inc 4 sts every 4th row as est 8 times more, then every other row 4 times—76 sts. Work 3 rows even.

Bind off 6 sts at beg of next 10 rows—16 sts. Work 2 rows even.

Shape gusset Dec 1 st each side every other row 4 times, then every 4th row once—6 sts. Work 5 rows even. Inc 1 st each side every 4th row 6 times—18 sts. Inc 1 st each side every other row 7 times—32 sts. Work 3 rows even. Place sts on a holder.

UPPER BODY

With RS facing and MC, pick up and k 37 sts evenly along top of left leg, k32 from gusset, then pick up and k37 sts evenly along right leg to top —106 sts. Work 3 rows St st, beg with a WS row.

Next row K35, k2tog, SKP, k28, k2tog, SKP, k35—102 sts. Work 3 rows even.

Next row K34, k2tog, SKP, k26, k2tog, SKP, k34—98 sts. Work 3 rows even.

Next row K33, k2tog, SKP, k24, k2tog, SKP, k33—94 sts. Work 3 rows even. Cont in St st, dec 4 sts every 4th row as established 5 times more—74 sts rem. Then dec 4 sts every other row 4 times—58 sts. Work 5 rows even.

Shape neck *Next row (RS)* K29, turn and cont on these 29 sts. Work 3 rows St st, AT SAME TIME, bind off 4 sts at beg of next 2 WS rows—21 sts.

Next row Knit.

Next row (WS) Bind off 4 sts, place marker (pm) for position of head frill, p to end—17 sts. Work 14 rows even. Dec 1 st at beg of next and every RS row until 13 sts rem, then dec 1 st from same edge every row 5 times—8 sts. Bind off. Join yarn to rem sts, bind off next 4 sts, k to end—25 sts. Work 1 row even. Work 3 rows St st, AT SAME TIME, bind off 4 sts at beg of every RS row twice—17 sts. Work 1 row, pm for head frill. Work 14 rows even. Dec 1 st at end of every RS row until 13 sts rem, then dec 1 st from same edge every row 5 times—8 sts. Bind off.

HEAD

With MC, cast on 40 sts. Work 2 rows St st, pm at each end of first row for head frill position. Cast on 5 sts at beg of next 6 rows—70 sts. Work 20 rows even.

Shape nose *Next row* [K3tog] 5 times, k40, [k3tog] 5 times—50 sts.

Next row Purl.

Next row K10, [k3tog] 10 times, k10—30 sts.

Next row Purl. Bind off 8 sts at beg of next 2 rows—14 sts. Dec 1 st at each end of every row until 4 sts rem.

Next row P4tog. Fasten off.

Head frill (make 2) With MC, cast on 12 sts. Work 2 rows St st. Cast on 4 sts at beg of next 2 rows, then 3 sts at beg of foll 2 rows—26 sts. Cast on 2 sts at beg of next 2 rows—30 sts. Inc 1 st at each side of next and every other row 3 times, then every 4th row once—38 sts. Work 3 rows even.

Divide for head *Next row* K13, turn and cont on these 13 sts. Dec 1 st at beg of next row, then at same edge in next 3 rows—9 sts. Work 1 row. Dec 1 st at end of next row—8 sts. Work 13 rows even, pm in last st of last row. Bind off. Join yarn to rem sts, bind off next 12 sts, k to end—13 sts. Dec 1 st at end of next row, then at same edge in next 3 rows—9 sts. Work 1 row even. Dec 1 st at beg of next row—8 sts. Work 13 rows, pm in first st of last row. Bind off.

ARMS (MAKE 2)

With B, cast on 18 sts. P 1 row, pm in center of row.

Next row K into front and back loop of every st—36 sts.

Continued on page 62

Next row Purl. Break off B. With MC, work 14 rows St st, pm in center of 8th row.

Next row K4, [k2tog, k1] 10 times, k2—26 sts. Inc 1 st each side every other row 8 times—42 sts. Work 11 rows even.

Shape top Bind off 4 sts at beg of next 2 rows—34 sts. Dec 1 st each side every other row twice, then every row 5 times—20 sts. Bind off.

Head frill border With RS facing, MC and beg at 2nd marker of one head frill piece, pick up and k 46 sts evenly down side edge to center of cast on edge, 1 st from center of cast on edge, then 46 sts to first marker—93 sts.

Row 1 Purl.

Row 2 Bind off 4 sts, *k5, bind off 3 sts, rep from * to last st. Place sts on holder.

HORNS

With RS facing and B, k across first set of 5 sts.

**Next row* P5, turn.

Next row K5, turn.

Next row P5 turn.

Next row SKP, k1, k2tog, turn.

Next row P3, turn.

Next row SKP. Pull yarn end through sts to secure.*** With RS facing, join B to next set of 5 sts. ** Rep between **'s 9 times, then work from ** to *** once (11 horns). Rep head frill border and horns on 2nd head frill piece.

Head horns (make 2) With MC, cast on 18 sts. K 1 row on WS. With B, work in St st, dec 1 st each side of 3rd row then every other row 7 times more—2 sts.

Next row K2tog. Pull yarn end through sts to secure.

Nose horn With MC, cast on 20 sts. K 1 row on WS. With B, work in St st, dec 1 st each side of 3rd row then every other row twice more—14 sts. Dec 1 st each side every row 6 times—2 sts.

Next row K2tog. Fasten off.

Tail Bumps (make 5) With C, cast on 7 sts. Work 3 rows garter st, dec 1 st each side on 2nd and 3rd rows. Cast off rem 3 sts.

FINISHING

With RS tog, back stitch 2 head frill pieces tog, leaving an opening at center of bound off edge. Turn head frill to RS. Stuff each horn,

secure with a small stitch on inside. Stuff rem of head frill lightly and close opening. Join straight underseam of head. Place a point at each end of nose to end of underseam, then sew shaped edges to bound off sts at end of nose. Join bound off sts at top of neck shaping on upper body. Place head frill markers on head to head frill markers on neck shaping of upper body. Pin head frill between markers. Sew head frill in place, working through all 4 thicknesses. Sew rem of head in place to neck shaping. Join back seam of each leg. Sew soles of feet to base of legs, matching top of soles to toes of feet. Sew side edges of gusset to side edge of thighs. Sew rem edges of gusset to bound off sts of legs. Sew tail into tail opening. Join tail seam. Join back seam of toy, leaving an opening at base. Stuff toy and close opening. Join side edges of head and nose horns and stuff. Sew horns to top of head and nose as pictured. Sew cast on edge of tail bumps evenly spaced along tail seam. Join arm seams. Join cast on edge of arms, matching marker at cast on edge to arm seam. Stuff arms. Sew a tight running st through both thicknesses of arm between marker at cast-on edge and 2nd marker. Sew tight running st halfway between first running sts and each edge of hand, to form 4 fingers. Sew top of arms to body. With D and stem st and satin st, embroider eyes to sides of head. Stem st nostrils to each side of nose and embroider mouth. Cut out different size circles from felt and glue to each thigh, tail and to front of head frill piece.

SWEATER

Back and front With A, cast on 61 sts.
Row 1 K2, *p1, k1; rep from *, k1.
Row 2 K1, *p1, k1; rep from * to end. Rep rows 1 and 2 once, dec 1 st in center of last row—60 sts. Work in St st, dec 1 st each side, alternating dec rows between every 3rd and every 4th row until 48 sts rem, then dec 1 st every other row 8 times—32 sts. Work 1 row. Place sts on holder.

Sleeves Cast on 35 sts. Work 4 rows rib as for

back. Work in St st, inc at each end of 3rd and foll alt rows until there are 45 sts. Work 9 rows. Bind off.

Neckband With RS facing, k across 32 sts on front holder, 32 sts on back holder, inc 1 st in center—65 sts. Work 11 rows rib as for back, beg with a Row 2. Bind off loosely in rib.

FINISHING

Back stitch shoulders tog, reversing seam on neckband for turn back. Fold neckband to RS and sew in place. Sew in sleeves. Sew side and sleeve seams.

This madcap moppet is up for anything!
Dynamic bands of contrasting color and flaming orange braids make this
hard-to-miss pal a standout. Just add a button face and a classy necktie and he's ready to roll.

bring in the funk

materials
Canadiana by Patons®,
3½oz/100g balls, each approx
228yds/205m (acrylic)
1 ball each in #3 Black (A),
#101 Winter White (B),
#5 Cardinal Red (C),
#72 Deep Orange (D) and
#120 Aqua Sea (E)
One pair size 5 (3.75mm) needles
OR SIZE TO OBTAIN GAUGE
Stitch holders and markers
Fiberfill
One ½"/13mm heart-shaped
red button for mouth
Two 1"/25mm round buttons
(one orange, one red) for eyes
Crochet hook (for attaching hair)
Yarn needle

FINISHED MEASUREMENTS

20"/51cm tall

12½"/32cm circumference

GAUGE

19 sts and 26 rows to 4"/10cm over St st using size 5 (3.75mm) needles.
TAKE TIME TO CHECK YOUR GAUGE.

STRIPE PAT

*1 row C, 3 rows B, 3 rows A, 1 row E, 3 rows B, 3 rows A, 1 row D, 3 rows B; 3 rows A; rep from * (21 rows) for Stripe Pat. (Note: Carry colors A and B up the side of the work; cut colors C, D, and E after working single row.)

ARMS (MAKE 2)

With A, cast on 20 sts. Beg with a k row, work in St st and Stripe Pat for 21 rows, then work rows 1-7 once more. Cut yarn. Place sts on hold.

LEFT LEG

With A, cast on 30 sts. Beg with a k row, work in St st and Stripe Pat for 21 rows, then work rows 1-18 once more. Cut yarn. Leave sts on needle.

Continued on page 66

Designed by Barbara Venishnick

bring in the funk

Continued from page 64

RIGHT LEG

With A, cast on 30 sts onto empty needle. Work as for left leg. Do not cut yarn after last row. Sts of both legs should end up on same needle.

Join legs *Next row (WS)* With A, p across 30 sts of each leg—60 sts.

BODY

With A, work 2 rows even. Work rows 1-21 of Stripe Pat, then rows 1-7 once more.

Join arms *Next row (RS)* With E, k15 sts from body (for ½ back), then k20 sts from one arm holder, bind off 1 body st, k to last 17 sts, bind off 1 st, k20 sts from 2nd arm holder, k rem 15 sts of body—98 sts. With B, purl.

Shoulder shaping *Dec row (RS)* With B, k12, k2tog, k1, place marker (pm), k1, ssk, k14, k2tog, k1, pm, k1, ssk, k22, k2tog, k1, pm, k1, ssk, k14, k2tog, k1, pm, k1, ssk, k12—90 sts. With B, purl. Cont in Stripe Pat as foll:

Next row (RS) *K to 3 sts before marker, k2tog, k1, sl marker, k1, ssk; rep from * 3 times more, k to end.

Next row Purl. Rep last 2 rows 6 times more, removing markers on last row—34 sts.

Neck shaping *Next row (RS)* K4, [k2tog, k2] twice, ssk, k6, [k2tog, k2] twice, ssk, k4—28 sts.

Next row Purl.

HEAD

Row 1 (RS) K7, [k into front, back, front] of next st (top of arm), k12, [k into front, back, front] of next st (top of arm), k7—32 sts.

Row 2 P8, M1, p1, M1, p14, M1, p1, M1, p8—36 sts.

Row 3 K9, M1, k1, M1, k16, M1, k1, M1, k9—40 sts.

Row 4 P10, M1, p1, M1, p18, M1, p1, M1, p10—44 sts.

Row 5 K11, M1, k1, M1, k20, M1, k1, M1, k11—48 sts.

Row 6 P12, M1, p1, M1, p22, M1, p1, M1, p12—52 sts. Work 18 rows even in Stripe Pat.

Shape top of head *Row 1* (RS) K12, S2KP, k22, S2KP, k12—48 sts.

Row 2 P11, p3tog, p20, p3tog, p11—44 sts.

Row 3 K10, S2KP, k18, S2KP, k10—40 sts.

Row 4 P9, p3tog, p16, p3tog, p9—36 sts.

Row 5 K8, S2KP, k14, S2KP, k8—32 sts.

Row 6 P7, p3tog, p12, p3tog, p7—28 sts. Bind off.

FOOT

With RS facing and A, pick up and k29 sts along cast-on edge of one leg.

Row 1 (WS) Purl.

Inc row (RS) K14, M1, k1 (mark this st for center top of foot), M1, k14. Cont in St st, inc 1 st each side of marked st every row 4 times—39 sts. Work 4 rows even.

Next row (WS) P1, p2tog, p15, p3tog, p15, p2tog, p1—35 sts. Bind off.

Rep for other foot.

HAND

With RS facing and A, pick up and k20 sts along cast-on edge of arm. Purl 1 row.

Inc row (RS) [K2, M1] 9 times, k2—29 sts. Work 6 rows even in St st.

Shape top of hand *Row 1 (WS)* [P2tog, p1] 9 times, p2tog—19 sts.

Row 2 [K2tog, k1] 6 times, k1—13 sts.

Row 3 [P2tog, p1] 4 times, p1—9 sts.

Row 4 [K2tog, k1] 3 times—6 sts.

Row 5 [P2tog] 3 times—3 sts. Cut yarn and draw through rem sts. Pull sts tog and fasten off. Rep for other hand.

FINISHING

Fold each foot and leg in half. Sew bottom bound-off edge and back seam of foot. Stuff foot firmly. Sew leg seam and stuff less firmly. Sew hand seam and stuff hand firmly. Sew arm seam and stuff less firmly. Sew ³/₄ of the way up the center back seam and stuff body less firmly, then sew rest of back seam to neck. Stuff head and close rem seam.

HAIR (MAKE 8 BRAIDS WITH C AND 7 WITH D)

Cut 9 strands of C each 6"/15.5cm long. Holding strands tog in a bundle, fold bundle in half. Insert crochet hook through 2 sts along side edge of head and pull center of bundle through. Cont pulling one end of bundle through to the other side of the head, holding the other bundle end firmly so that it stays in place. Adjust both ends of bundle so that they are equal in length. Separate the resulting 18 strands into 3 groups of 6 strands each. Braid strands tog and tie end of braid firmly with A. Trim ends about ³/₄"/2cm above tie. Attach rem braids, alternating colors (see photo). Sew on buttons for eyes and mouth.

BOW TIE

With E, cast on 7 sts. K 10 rows.

Next row K2, S2KP, k2—5 sts. K 1 row.

Next row K1, S2KP, k1—3 sts. K 63 rows.

Next row (RS) [K1, M1] twice, k1—5 sts. K 1 row.

Next row K2, M1, k1, M1, k2—7 sts. K 10 rows. Bind off. Wrap bow tie around doll's neck and overlap wide ends. Tie ends tog by wrapping a strand of A several times around center.

You don't have to head down to Antarctica to enjoy the company
of a few good penguins. With pure white torsos, noble beaks, and inquisitive eyes,
these cold-weather cuties are a pleasure to whip up.

southern exposure

materials
Cleckheaton Country 8-Ply
by Plymouth Yarns, 1¾oz/50g skeins,
each approx 105yds/96m (wool)
2 skeins in #0006 Black (MC) and
1 skein in #0003 White (C1)
Small amounts of #1857 Gold (C2)
and #1884 Yellow (C3)
One pair size 3 (3mm) needles
OR SIZE TO OBTAIN GAUGE
Two ³⁄₈"/10mm sew-on eyes
Fiberfill

FINISHED MEASUREMENTS

12"/30.5cm tall

GAUGE

28 sts and 38 rows to 4"/10cm over St st with MC using size 3 (3mm) needles.

TAKE TIME TO CHECK YOUR GAUGE.

BODY

BACK

With MC, cast on 5 sts. K 1 row, p 1 row.

Row 3 Inc 1 st, k to last 2 sts, inc 1 st, k1—7 sts.

Row 4 and all WS rows Purl.

Rows 5 and 7 Rep row 3.

Row 9 [Inc 1 st, k2] 3 times, inc 1 st, k1—15 sts.

Rows 11, 15, and 19 Rep row 3.

Row 13 [Inc 1 st, k4] 3 times, inc1 st, k1—21 sts.

Row 17 [Inc 1 st, k6] 3 times, inc 1 st, k1—27 sts.

Row 21 [Inc 1 st, k8] 3 times, inc 1 st, k1—33 sts. Cont to work in St st, rep row 3

every 4 rows until 39 sts. Work 35 rows even. Mark each end of last row for

position of flippers.

Next row K1, [k2tog, k3] 4 times, [SKP, k3] 3 times, SKP, k1—31 sts.

Designed by Cleckheaton Studio

Continued on page 70

Work 3 rows even.

Next row K1, [k2tog, k2] 3 times, k2tog, k1, [SKP, k2] 3 times, SKP, k1—23 sts. Work 3 rows even.

Head shaping *Next row* K6, [inc in next st, k2] 3 times, inc in next st, k7—27 sts. P 1 row.

Note To turn, bring yarn to front of work, sl 1, yarn to back of work, sl same st back to LH needle, then turn work.

Rows 79 and 80 Work to last 4 sts, turn.

Rows 81 and 82 Work to last 8 sts, turn.

Rows 83 and 84 Work even in St st on all sts. Rep last 6 rows 4 more times.

Row 109 K1, k2tog, k4, k2tog, k9, SKP, k4, SKP, k1.

Row 110 and all WS rows Purl.

Row 111 K1, k2tog, k3, k2tog, k7, SKP, k3, SKP, k1.

Row 113 K1, k2tog, k2, k2tog, k5, SKP, k2, SKP, k1.

Row 115 K1, k2tog, k1, k2tog, k3, SKP, k1, SKP, k1—11 sts. Cast on 3 sts for beak.

Row 117 K4, [k2tog] twice, k1, [SKP] twice, k1, turn, cast on 3 sts—13 sts.

Row 119 Knit.

Row 121 K5, sl 2, k1, p2sso, k5—11 sts.

Row 123 K4, sl 2, k1, p2sso, k4—9 sts.

Row 125 K3, sl 2, k1, p2sso, k3—7 sts.

Row 127 K2, sl 2, k1, p2sso, k2—5 sts. P 1 row.

Cut yarn, leaving a long end. Draw end through rem sts and gather tightly tog. Fasten off. Sew beak seam.

FRONT

With C1, cast on 5 sts. Work as for body back through row 7. Cont in St st, inc as in row 3 every other row once, every 4th row twice—17 sts. P 1 row.

Row 19 K3, bind off 3 sts for leg opening, k5, bind off 3 sts, k3.

Row 20 P3, turn; cast on 6 sts, turn; p5 turn; cast on 6 sts, turn; p3—23 sts. Cont in St st, inc as in row 3 at each end of next and foll 4th row—27 sts. Work 25 rows even. Dec row 51 K1, k2tog, k to last 3 sts, SKP, k1. Rep dec row every 6 rows 3 times—19 sts. Work 3 rows even.

Row 73 [K1, k2tog] 3 times, [k1, SKP] 3 times, k1—13 sts. Work 3 rows even.

Next row K4, turn; p4.

Next row K across all sts.

Next row P4, turn; k4.

Next row P across all sts. Rep last 4 rows twice. Cont in St st, rep row 51 every other row 4 times—5 sts. Work 1 row even. Bind off. With MC, duplicate st underside of neck and face. With C3, duplicate st from top of flippers to underside of neck. With C4, duplicate st a few places randomly on chest. (See photo) Sew front body to back, with bound-off sts of front body at cast-on sts of beak, leaving an opening for stuffing. Stuff firmly, finish sewing closed.

FEET (MAKE 2)

With MC, cast on 6 sts. ***Beg with a k row, work 4 rows in St st.

Row 5 *[Insert needle into next st and into corresponding lp of cast-on edge and k these 2 sts tog—tuck made] twice, pass first st over st just worked; rep from * to last st, k1 —2 sts. *** *Row 6* P2, turn; cast on 5 sts—7 sts. Rep from *** to *** once.

Next row P2, turn; cast on 4 sts—6 sts. Rep from *** to ***once. Pass first st over last; working along top edge of 'claws', pick up and p 6 sts (1 in top of each 'claw' and 1 in-between each)— 7 sts. Beg with a k row, work 5 rows in St st.

Next row P1, p2tog tbl, p1, p2tog, p1. Bind off. With MC, cast on 5 sts, turn; with RS of 'claws' facing, pick up and k 6 sts from base of picked-up sts of foot, turn; cast on 5 sts—16 sts.

Next row P5, p2tog, p2, p2tog tbl, p5—14 sts. Work 4 rows in St st. Bind off. Sew back seam of leg, then tack foot to base of leg. Stuff firmly, then sew to front body at leg holes, adding additional stuffing to body if necessary.

Upper right flipper With MC, cast on 24 sts.

Row 1 K, inc in last st.

Row 2 Inc in first st, p to end. Rep last 2 rows 3 times—32 sts. Mark beg of last row for top edge.

Row 9 K2tog, k to end.

Row 10 and all WS rows P to last 2 sts, p2tog.

Row 11 Bind off 2 sts, k to end.

Row 13 Bind off 3 sts, k to end.

Row 15 Bind off 4 sts, k to end.

Row 17 Bind off 11 sts, k to end—7 sts.

Rows 19 and 21 Rep row 9.

Row 23 K2tog twice. Fasten off.

Upper left flipper Work as for upper right flipper, reversing shaping.

Under flippers With C1, work as for upper right and left flippers.

FINISHING

Sew pairs of flippers tog. Block flippers to flatten. Foll photo, sew flippers to body, with front of top edge at markers. Mark position, then sew on eyes, stitching back and forth through head to secure.

Bring this beloved plant dweller down to earth in a rainbow of hues.
It's just a matter of crocheted discs, a little elastic cording, and voilà!
This caterpillar is a wrap.

not-so-creepy crawly

materials
Nature Spun by Brown Sheep Yarn Co.,
3½ oz/100g balls, each approx
245yds/220m (wool)
1 ball each in #N54 Orange You Glad (A),
#N24 Evergreen (B), #N46 Red Fox (C),
#305 Impasse Yellow (D),
#N36 China Blue (E) and
#N65 Sapphire (F)
Size I/9 (5.5mm) crochet hook
OR SIZE TO OBTAIN GAUGE
Fiberfill
1 yd/1m of ¼"/.5cm elastic cord and
one ⅝"/15mm purple button
Yarn needle

FINISHED MEASUREMENTS

Approx 17"/43cm long

GAUGE

One circle to 2½"/6.5cm using size I/9 (5.5mm) hook.
TAKE TIME TO CHECK YOUR GAUGE.

NOTE

To dec 1 sc, [insert hook into next st and draw up a lp] twice, yo and draw
through all 3 lps on hook.

Designed by Sandi Prosser

Ch 5. Join ch with a sl st forming a ring.

Rnd 1 Ch 3 (always counts as 1 dc), work 14 dc in ring—15 dc. Join rnd with a sl st in 3rd ch of ch-3.

Rnd 2 Ch 3, 1 dc in same sp as sl st, work 2 dc in each st around—30 dc. Join rnd with a sl st in 3rd ch of ch-3. Fasten off.

HEAD

With MC, ch 3. Join ch with a sl st forming a ring.

Rnd 1 Ch 1 (always counts as 1 sc), work 5 sc in ring—6 sc. Join this rnd and all rem rnds with a sl st in ch-1.

Rnd 2 Ch 1, 1 sc in same sp as sl st, work 2 sc in each st around—12 sc.

Rnd 3 Ch 1, 1 sc in same sp as sl st, 1 sc in next st, *work 2 sc in next st, 1 sc in next st; rep from * around—18 sc.

Rnd 4 Ch 1, 1 sc in same sp as sl st, 1 sc in each of next 2 sts, *work 2 sc in next st, 1 sc in each of next 2 sts; rep from * around—24 sc.

Rnd 5 Ch 1, 1 sc in same sp as sl st, 1 sc in each of next 3 sts, *work 2 sc in next st, 1 sc in each of next 3 sts; rep from * around—30 sc.

Rnd 6 Ch 1, 1 sc in same sp as sl st, 1 sc in each of next 4 sts, *work 2 sc in next st, 1 sc in each of next 4 sts; rep from * around—36 sc.

Rnd 7 Ch 1, 1 sc in same sp as sl st, 1 sc in each of next 5 sts, *work 2 sc in next st, 1 sc in each of next 5 sts; rep from * around—42 sc.

Rnds 8-15 Ch 1, 1 sc in each st around.

Rnd 16 Ch 1, *dec 1 sc over next 2 sts, 1 sc in each of next 5 sts; rep from * around—36 sc.

Rnd 17 Ch 1, *dec 1 sc over next 2 sts, 1 sc in each of next 4 sts; rep from * around—30 sc.

Rnd 18 Ch 1, *dec 1 sc over next 2 sts, 1 sc in each of next 3 sts; rep from * around—24 sc.

Rnd 19 Ch 1, *dec 1 sc over next 2 sts, 1 sc in each of next 2 sts; rep from * around—18 sc.

Rnd 20 Ch 1, *dec 1 sc over next 2 sts, 1 sc in next st; rep from * around—12 sc. Fasten off.

ANTENNA (MAKE 2)

With F, ch 21. Work 3 sc in 2nd ch from hook, then in each ch to end. Fasten off.

FINISHING

Stuff head with fiberfill; sew bottom opening closed. With F, embroider face as shown in photo. Sew antenna on head.

ASSEMBLY

Cut elastic 33"/84cm in length. Secure end of elastic to bottom of head with a few small back stitches. Thread circles from RS in the foll sequence (making sure to keep elastic cord relaxed): 5 each B, C, D, E, A, F, B, C, D, E, A, F. Thread button onto elastic. Thread elastic back through all circles and secure to bottom of head with a few small back stitches.

This is one squirrel that won't have to forage for food!
Our furry fellow has fuzzy tweed fur, while an unruly loop stitch
shapes his trademark bushy tail.

what a
nut

materials
Divine by Patons®, 3½oz/100g balls,
each approx 142yds/128m
(acrylic/mohair/polyester)
3 balls in #06013 Deep Earth (MC) and
1 ball in #06011 Soft Heather (A)
Canadiana by Patons®, 3½oz/100g
balls, each approx 215yds/194m
(acrylic)
1 ball in #304 Beige (B) and
5yds in #3 Black (C)
One pair each sizes 5 and 7
(3.75 and 4.5mm) needles
OR SIZE TO OBTAIN GAUGE
One set (4) size 7 (4.5mm) double-
pointed needles (dpns)
Fiberfill
2 black buttons for eyes
Yarn needle
Split-coil stitch markers (several
different colors)
Stitch holder
2 pipe cleaners

Designed by Svetlana Avrakh

FINISHED MEASUREMENTS

18"/45.5cm tall

GAUGE

16 sts and 20 rows to 4"/10cm over St st with MC using larger needles.
TAKE TIME TO CHECK YOUR GAUGE.

LOOP STITCH PATTERN

Row 1 (WS) **Purl.**

Row 2 K1, *k1, do not drop st from LH needle, bring yarn to front, wrap yarn clockwise around left thumb, bring yarn to back, sl st just made from RH needle to LH needle and k2tog (loop made); rep from* to last st, k1. Rep rows 1 and 2 for Loop Stitch Pattern.

BODY BACK

Left side With larger needles and MC, cast on 30 sts. Work 5 rows in St st.

Next row (WS) **Bind off 12 sts** (place yellow marker on st after bind-off), p to end of row—18 sts. Break MC.

Right side With larger needles and MC, cast on 30 sts, placing 2 red markers at each end of cast-on row. Work 6 rows in St st. Join pieces

Next row (RS) **Bind off 12 sts** (place yellow marker on st after bind-off), k to end of row, cast on 28 sts onto RH needle, then k across 18 sts of left side—64 sts.

Continued on page 76

w h a t   a   n u t

Continued from page 74

Beg with a p row, work 23 rows in St st. Dec 1 st each side on next row—62 sts. Work 1 row even. Dec 1 st each side on next 5 rows—52 sts. Work 1 row even.

Beg short-row shaping (Note SI sts purlwise with yarn at WS of work.)

Row 1 (RS) K42, turn, leave rem 10 sts unworked.

Row 2 (WS) P32, turn, leave rem 10 sts unworked.

Row 3 SI 1, k32, turn, leave rem 9 sts unworked.

Row 4 SI 1, p33, turn, leave rem 9 sts unworked.

Row 5 SI 1, k34, turn, leave rem 8 sts unworked.

Row 6 SI 1, p35, turn, leave rem 8 sts unworked.

Row 7 SI 1, k36, turn, leave rem 7 sts unworked.

Row 8 SI 1, p37, turn, leave rem 7 sts unworked.

Row 9 SI 1, k38, turn, leave rem 6 sts unworked.

Row 10 SI 1, p39, turn, leave rem 6 sts unworked.

Row 11 SI 1, k40, turn, leave rem 5 sts unworked.

Row 12 SI 1, p41, turn, leave rem 5 sts unworked.

Row 13 SI 1, k to end of row.

Row 14 P52. Place white marker on sts at each end of needle.

Shape upper back (Note SI center marker every row.)

Next row (RS) K22, k2tog, k2, place center marker, k2, ssk, k22—50 sts.

Next row Purl.

Next row K to 4 sts before marker, k2tog, k4, ssk, k to end—48 sts.

Next row Purl.

Next row (RS) Inc 1 st in first st, k to 4 sts before marker, k2tog, k4, ssk, k to last 2 sts, inc 1 st in next st, k1. Rep last 2 rows 5 times more.

Next row (WS) Purl.

Next row K to 4 sts before marker, k2tog, k4, ssk, k to end. Rep last 2 rows twice more—42 sts. Place blue marker on sts at each end of needle.

Next row (WS) Purl.

Next row K1, ssk, k to 4 sts before marker, k2tog, k4, ssk, k to last 3 sts, k2tog, k1. Rep last 2 rows once more—34 sts.

Next row Purl.

Next row K1, ssk, k to last 3 sts, k2tog, k1. Rep

last 2 rows twice more—28 sts. Beg with a purl row, work 5 rows in St st.

Shape head *Row 1 (RS)* K11, k2tog, k2, ssk, k3, turn, leave rem 8 sts unworked.

Row 2 SI 1, p9, turn, leave rem 8 sts unworked.

Row 3 SI 1, k1, k2tog, k2, ssk, k3, turn, leave rem 7 sts unworked.

Row 4 SI 1, p9, turn, leave rem 7 sts unworked.

Row 5 SI 1, k1, k2tog, k2, ssk, k3, turn, leave rem 6 sts unworked.

Row 6 SI 1, p9, turn, leave rem 6 sts unworked.

Row 7 SI 1, k1, k2tog, k2, ssk, k3, turn, leave rem 5 sts unworked.

Row 8 SI 1, p9, turn, leave rem 5 sts unworked.

Row 9 SI 1, k1, k2tog, k2, ssk, k3, turn, leave rem 4 sts unworked.

Row 10 SI 1, p9, turn, leave rem 4 sts unworked.

Row 11 SI 1, k1, k2tog, k2, ssk, k to end of row.

Row 12 P16. Place black marker at each end of row.

Rows 13 and 15 SI 1, k to 3 sts before marker, k2tog, k2, ssk, k to end.

Row 14 P14.

Row 16 P12. Dec 1 st each side on next row,

then every 4th row 3 times more—4 sts. Work 1 row even. Bind off. Place orange marker at each end of row.

BELLY AND FRONT OF HEAD

With larger needles and A, cast on 6 sts. Place red marker at each end of row. Work 2 rows in St st.

Next row (WS) Inc 1 st in first st, k to last 2 sts, inc 1 st in next st, k1.

Next row Purl. Rep last 2 rows 7 times more—22 sts. Work 2 rows even. Dec 1 st each side on next row, then every other row 5 times more—10 sts. Place yellow marker at each end of row. Beg with a purl row, work 15 rows in St st. Inc 1 st each side every row 7 times. Work 1 row even. Inc 1 st each side on next row—26 sts. Place white marker on sts at each end of needle. Beg with a purl row, work 5 rows in St st. Dec 1 st each side on next row, then every other row 5 times more—14 sts. Beg with a purl row, work 5 rows in St st. Place a blue marker at each end of row.

Next row (RS) Inc 1 st in first st, k to last 2 sts, inc 1 st in next st, k1.

Next row Purl. Rep last 2 rows 4 times more—24 sts.

Next row (RS) Inc 1 st in first st, k9, place orange marker on last st, turn, leave rem 14 sts on a holder—11 sts.

Next row Purl.

Next row Inc 1 st in first st, k7, k2tog, k1.

Next row Purl.

Next row K to last 3 sts, k2tog, k1.

Next row Purl. Rep last 2 rows 3 times more—7 sts. Bind off. Place black marker on last st of row. Place 14 sts on holder onto needle, ready to work a RS row.

Next row (RS) Join A and bind off 4 sts, place orange marker on last st after bind-off, k to last 2 sts, inc 1 st in next st, k1—11 sts.

Next row Purl.

Next row K1, ssk, k to last 2 sts, inc 1 st in next st, k1.

Next row Purl.

Next row K1, ssk, k to end—10 sts.

Next row Purl. Rep last 2 rows 3 times more—7 sts. Place black marker on last st of last row. Bind off. Sew back and front pieces tog, matching colors of markers and leaving an opening at bottom for stuffing. Stuff toy firmly, shaping body as shown in photo. Sew opening closed.

LOWER PAWS

With dpns and MC, cast on 16 sts, divided over 3 needles as foll: 5/5/6. K 6 rnds.

Inc rnd [K1, M1, k6, M1, k1] twice—20 sts. K 6 rnds.

Inc rnd [K1, M1, k8, M1, k1] twice—24 sts. K 6 rnds.

Inc rnd [K1, M1, k10, M1, k1] twice—28 sts. K 3 rnds.

Dec rnd [K1, ssk, k8, k2tog, k1] twice—24 sts.

Continued on page 78

77

what a nut

Continued from page 77

Dec rnd [K1, ssk, k6, k2tog, k1] twice—20 sts.

Dec rnd [K1, ssk, k4, k2tog, k1] twice—16 sts. Rearrange sts on needles as foll: Sl first 3 sts from 2nd needle onto first needle, sl last 2 sts from 2nd needle onto 3rd needle. Graft 8 sts from one needle tog with 8 sts from other needle. Stuff paw lightly. With MC, work back stitch across paw 1"/2.5cm in from front edge. With C, embroider claws by taking yarn once around end of paw for each claw. Sew paws onto body.

RIGHT UPPER PAW

(*Note* When working with 2 colors, twist yarns on WS at color change to prevent holes in work.) With larger needles and MC, cast on 12 sts. Work in St st, inc 1 st each side on 3rd row, then every 4th row twice more—18 sts. Work 1 row even.

Next row (RS) K to end of row, then join A and cast on 10 sts—28 sts. Beg with a purl row, work 15 rows even in St st, matching colors.

Dec row (RS) [K2, k2tog] 7 times—21 sts. Work 12 rows even in St st, matching colors.

Next row (WS) Bind off 9 sts, then with MC, p to end—12 sts. Break A. With MC, work 3 rows even.

Next row (WS) [P2, p2tog] 3 times—9 sts. Bind off.

LEFT UPPER PAW

With larger needles and MC, cast on 12 sts. Work in St st, inc 1 st each side on 3rd row, then every 4th row twice more—18 sts.

Next row (WS) P to end of row, then join A and cast on 10 sts—28 sts. Beg with a knit row, work 16 rows even in St st, matching colors.

Dec row (RS) [K2tog, k2] 7 times—21 sts. Work 11 rows even in St st, matching colors.

Next row (RS) Bind off 9 sts, then with MC, k to end—12 sts. Break A. With MC, work 4 rows even.

Next row (WS) [P2, p2tog] 3 times—9 sts. Bind off. Sew side and top seam. Stuff paws firmly. Sew onto body, with A portion to inside. With C, embroider claws.

EARS (MAKE 2)

With larger needles and MC, cast on 10 sts. Work in St st, dec 1 st each side on 3rd row, then every 4th row 3 times—2 sts.

Next row Purl. Inc 1 st each side on next row, then every 4th row 3 times more—10 sts. Work 2 rows even. Bind off. Sew back and front of ear tog. Sew ears to head. With C, embroider nose and mouth, using photo as guide. Sew on buttons for eyes.

TAIL

Back With larger needles and MC, cast on 4 sts (tip of tail). Work Loop Stitch Pattern for 10 rows. Cont in pat, inc 1 st each side on next row, then every other row 3 times more. Work 3 rows even. Inc 1 st each side on next row—14 sts. Work even until piece measures 19"/48cm from beg, end with a WS row. Bind off.

Front Work as for back until piece measures 7"/18cm from beg, end with a WS row. Bind off. Sew back and front tog, matching cast-on edges and placing pipe cleaners along seams (so tail will bend). Sew single side of back tail to back of body, stuffing lightly as you sew.

NUT

With smaller needles and B, cast on 19 sts. Beg Seed St:

Row 1 (RS) K1, *p1, k1; rep from * to end. K the purl sts and p the knit sts. Rep last row 16 times more.

Next row (WS) K1, [k2tog, k1] 6 times—13 sts.

Next row Knit.

Next row K1, [k2tog] 6 times—7 sts.

Next row Knit. Break yarn, leaving a long end. Thread yarn through rem sts and tighten up. Sew side seam. Stuff nut firmly. Pick up sts along cast-on edge and tighten. Sew nut between upper paws.

Warm, upbeat shades and a congenial grin make this gentle giant a cheery companion for all ages. All it takes is basic garter stitch and distinguishing blue birthmarks to make this extinct creature come to life.

bright
brontosaurus

materials
Astra by Patons®, 1¾oz/50g skein, each
approx 178yds/163m (acrylic)
1 skein in Pink #2211 (MC),
1 skein each of #2874 Yellow (A)
and #2751 White (B)
Small amount of #2765 Black (C)
One pair size 5 (3.75mm) needles
OR SIZE TO OBTAIN GAUGE
Fiberfill
Blue felt
Craft glue
Yarn needle

FINISHED MEASUREMENTS

18"/46cm tall.

GAUGE

23 sts and 31 rows to 4"/10cm over St st, using size 5 (3.75mm) needles.

TAKE TIME TO CHECK YOUR GAUGE.

STITCH GLOSSARY

SK2P Sl 1, k2tog, pass sl st over.

NOTES

When changing colors in the middle of a row, twist the color to be used (on WS) underneath and to the right of the color just used. Use a separate ball of yarn for each section of color. When binding off, the last st on RH needle is the first st of the stitch count that directly follows.

LEFT LEG

Sole **With A, cast on 7 sts.

Row 1 (RS) Knit. Work in garter st, inc 1 st each side of every row 4 times, then every other row twice—19 sts. Work even until piece measures 4¼"/11cm from beg, end with a RS row.

Next row (WS) With B, work in St st, dec 1 st each side of 4th row, then every other row twice more, then every row 3 times. Bind off rem 7 sts.

Continued on page 82

bright brontosaurus

Continued from page 80

Top of foot *Cast on* 92 sts as foll: 32 sts MC, 28 sts B, 32 sts MC. K 1 row, p 1 row, matching colors.**

Shape toes *Row 3* K32 MC, *(SKP, k4, k2tog) B, k2 MC; rep from * once, k8 B, k32 MC—88 sts.

Row 4 P32 MC, (p2tog, p4, p2tog tbl) B, *p2 MC, (p2tog, p2, p2tog tbl) B; rep from * once, p32 MC—82 sts.

Row 5 (K31, M1, k1) MC, *(SKP, k2tog) B, (k1, M1, k1) MC; rep from * once, k6 B, (k1, M1, k31) MC—82 sts.

Row 6 P33 MC, (p2tog, p2, p2tog tbl) B, p43 MC—80 sts.

Row 7 K43 MC, (SKP, k2tog) B, k33 MC—78 sts.

***With MC, work 5 rows St st, beg with a purl row.

Shape ankle *Next row* K24, (k3tog) 10 times, k24—58 sts. Work 9 rows even.

Next row K26, (M1, k2) 3 times, M1, k26—62 sts.

Next row Purl.

Next row K25, M1, k3, M1, k6, M1, k3, M1, k25—66 sts.*** Work 6 rows even.

Next row (WS) Bind off 33 sts, p to end—33 sts.

Shape thigh and tail opening *Row 1* Bind off 4 sts, k6, [M1, k7] 3 times, k1—32 sts.

Row 2 and all WS rows Purl.

Row 3 Bind off 4 sts, [M1, k8] 3 times, k3—31 sts.

Row 5 Bind off 2 sts, k1, [M1, k9] 3 times—32 sts.

Row 7 Bind off 2 sts, k5, [M1, k10] twice, k4, 32 sts.

Row 9 Bind off 2 sts, k1, [M1, k7] twice, k14, 32 sts.

Row 10 Purl. Work 9 rows even. Bind off 4 sts at beg of next and every WS row 3 times—20 sts.

Next row (RS) Cast on 2 sts, k to end—22 sts.

Next row Bind off 4 sts, p to end—18 sts.

Next row Cast on 4 sts, k to end—22 sts. Rep last 2 rows once, then first of these 2 rows once.

Next row Knit. Bind off 4 sts at beg of next and every WS row 3 times. Work 1 row even. Bind off rem 6 sts.

RIGHT LEG

Work as for left leg from ** to **.

Shape toes *Row 3* K32 MC, k8 B, *k2 MC, (SKP, K4, k2tog) B; rep from * once more, k32 MC—88 sts.

Row 4 P32 MC, *(p2tog, p2, p2tog tbl) B, p2 MC; rep from * once more, (p2tog, p4, p2tog tbl) B, p32 MC—82 sts.

Row 5 (K31, M1, k1) MC, k6 B, (k1, M1, k1) MC, *(SKP, k2tog) B, (k1, M1, k1) MC; rep from * once, k30 MC—82 sts.

Row 6 P43 MC, (p2tog, p2, p2tog tbl) B, p33 MC—80 sts.

Row 7 K33 MC, (SKP, K2tog) B, k43 MC—78 sts. Work as for left leg from *** to ***. Work 7 rows even.

Shape thigh and tail opening *Row 1* Bind off 33 sts, k7, (M1, k7) 3 times, k4—36 sts.

Row 2 Bind off 4 sts, p to end.

Row 3 K12, (M1, k8) twice, M1, k4—35 sts.

Row 4 Rep Row 2.

Row 5 (K9, M1) 3 times, k4—34 sts.

Row 6 Bind off 2 sts, p to end.

Row 7 K14, M1, k10, M1, k8—34 sts.

Row 8 Rep row 6.

Row 9 K21, M1, k7, M1, k4—34 sts.

Row 10 Bind off 2 sts, p to end—32 sts. Work 10 rows even. Bind off 4 sts at beg of next and every RS row 3 times—20 sts.

Next row (WS) Cast on 2 sts, p to end—22 sts.

Next row Bind off 4 sts, k to end—18 sts.

Next row Cast on 4 sts, p to end—22 sts. Rep last 2

rows once, then first of these 2 rows once more. *Next row* Purl. Bind off 4 sts at beg of next and every RS row 3 times. Work 1 row even. Bind off rem 6 sts.

TAIL

Cast on 10 sts as foll: 3 sts MC, 4 sts A, 3 sts MC.
Row 1 K3 MC, k4 A, k3 MC. [K 1 row, p 1 row matching colors] 3 times.
Row 7 (K2, M1, k1) MC, (k1, M1, k2, M1, k1) A, (k1, M1, k2) MC—14 sts. Work 5 rows even.
Row 13 (K3, M1, k1) MC, (k1, M1, k4, M1, k1) A, (k1, M1, k3) MC—18 sts. Work 5 rows even.
Row 19 (K3, [M1, k1] twice) MC, (k1, M1, k6, M1, k1) A, ([k1, M1] twice, k3) MC—24 sts. Work 5 rows even.
Row 25 (K4, M1, k2, M1, k1) MC, (k1, M1, k8, M1, k1) A, (k1, M1, k2, M1, k4) MC—30 sts. Work 5 rows even.
Row 31 (K5, M1, k3, M1, k1) MC, (k1, M1, k10, M1, k1) A, (k1, M1, k3, M1, k5) MC—36 sts. Work 3 rows even.
Row 35 (K6, M1, k4, M1, k1) MC, (k1, M1, k12, M1,

k1) A, (k1, M1, k4, M1, k6) MC—42 sts. Work 3 rows even.
Row 39 (K7, M1, k5, M1, k1) MC, (k1, M1, k14, M1, k1) A, (k1, M1, k5, M1, k7) MC—48 sts. Work 3 rows even. Cont to inc 6 sts every 4th row as established 6 more times—84 sts. Work 3 rows even.
Next row (K2, M1, [K12, M1] twice, k1) MC, (K1, M1, k28, M1, k1) B, (k1, M1, [k12, M1] twice, k2) MC—92 sts. Work 3 rows even. Keeping colors correct, bind off 6 sts at beg of next 10 rows—32 sts.

Shape gusset *Next row* With B, k1, SKP, k to last 3 sts, k2tog, k1—30 sts.
Next row Purl.
Next row K1, SK2P, k to last 4 sts, k3tog, k1—26 sts.
Next row Purl. Rep last 2 rows until 6 sts rem. Work 5 rows even. Cont in St st, inc 1 st each side every other row 13 times, then every 4th row twice—36 sts. Work 7 rows even. Place sts on holder.

Using back stitch, sew gusset to front of thighs, matching top edges. Sew rem of gusset to bound-off sts of legs. With MC, pick up and k 42 sts evenly across top of shaped edge of left leg, with A, k across 36 sts from holder, with MC, pick up and k 42 sts evenly across top of shaped edge of right leg—120 sts. Keeping colors correct, work 3 rows St st, beg with a purl row.

Shape body *Row 1* (K40, k2tog) MC, (SKP, k32, k2tog) A, (SKP, k40) MC—116 sts.
Row 2 and all WS rows Purl.
Row 3 (K38, k3tog) MC, k34 A, (SK2P, k38) MC—112 sts.
Row 5 (K37, k2tog) MC, (SKP, k30, k2tog) A, (SKP, k37) MC—108 sts.
Row 7 (K35, k3tog) MC, k32 A, (SK2P, k35) MC—104 sts.
Row 9 (K34, k2tog) MC, (SKP, k28, k2tog) A, (SKP, k34) MC—100 sts.
Row 11 (K32, k3tog) MC, k30 A, (SK2P, k32) MC—96 sts.
Row 13 (K31, k2tog) MC, (SKP, k26, k2tog) A, (SKP, k31) MC—92 sts.

Continued on page 84

bright brontosaurus

Continued from page 83

Row 15 (K29, k3tog) MC, k28 A, (SK2P, k29) MC—88 sts. Work 7 more rows, AT SAME TIME, cont to dec 4 sts every RS row as established, in colors as established.

Row 23 (SKP, k22, k2tog) MC, k24 A, (SKP, k22, k2tog) MC—72 sts.

Row 25 (K22, k2tog) MC, (SKP, k20, k2tog) A, (SKP, k22) MC—68 sts.

Row 27 (SKP, k19, k2tog) MC, k22 A, (SKP, k19, k2tog) MC—64 sts.

Row 29 (K19, k2tog) MC, (SKP, k18, k2tog) A, (SKP, k19) MC—60 sts.

Row 31 (SKP, k16, k2tog) MC, k20 A, (SKP, k16, k2tog) MC—56 sts.

Row 33 K18 MC, (SKP, k16, k2tog) A, k18 MC—54 sts.

Row 35 (SKP, k16) MC, k18 A, (k16, k2tog) MC—52 sts. Work 19 rows more, cont to dec 2 sts every other row as est in last 4 rows.

Row 55 (SKP, k11) MC, k8 A, (k11, k2tog) MC—32 sts.

Row 57 (SKP, k10) MC, k8 A, (k10, k2tog) MC—30 sts.

Row 59 (SKP, k9) MC, k8 A, (k9, k2tog) MC—28 sts.

Row 60 Purl. Work 10 rows even.

Shape Neck *Next row* K10 MC, turn and cont on these 10 sts. Dec 1 st at beg of next row, then dec 1 st at same edge every row 4 times more, then every other row 3 times—2 sts. *Next row* K2tog. Fasten off. Join A to rem sts, bind off next 8 sts, with MC, k to end—10 sts. With MC, cont on last 10 sts and complete to correspond with other side. Form neck into a tube, then stitch tog top of shaping where last st was fastened off at each side of neck.

HEAD

With MC, cast on 4 sts, pick up and k 14 sts evenly along right side of neck to top of shaping, 14 sts down left side of neck, then cast on 4 sts—36 sts.

Next row Purl.

Next row Inc once in each of next 4 sts, k28, inc once in each of next 4 sts—44 sts. Work 11 rows St st, beg with a WS row.

Next row K12, [k2tog] 10 times, k12—34 sts.

Next row Purl.

Next row K9, k2tog, [k3tog] 4 times, k2tog, k9—24 sts. Work 7 rows even.

Next row [K2tog] 12 times—12 sts.

Next row Purl. Break yarn, run thread through rem sts and draw tightly. Fasten off.

ARMS (MAKE 2)

With B, cast on 18 sts. P 1 row.

Next row K into front and back of each st—36 sts.

Next row P15, pm in last st for end of finger, p18, pm in last st for end of finger, p3. With MC, work 7 rows St st.

Next row P15, pm in last st for beg of finger, p18, pm in last st for beg of finger, p3. Work 2 rows.

Next row K2 MC, k3 A, k31 MC.

Next row P30 MC, p5 A, p1 MC.

Next row K7 A, k29 MC.

Next row P29 MC, p7 A. Rep last 2 rows twice more, then first of these 2 rows once.

Next row (P2, [p2tog, p2] 6 times, p3) MC, p7 A—30 sts. Work 18 rows even keeping established colors.

Shape shoulder *Next row* With A, bind off 7 sts, with MC, k to end—23 sts.

Next row With MC, purl. Dec 1 st at each side every other row twice, then every row 5 times—9 sts. Bind off.

FINISHING

Join head under chin. Sew cast-on sts of head to bound-off sts of neck. Join back seam of legs. Sew soles to base of legs, matching top of soles to toes of legs. Join tail seam. Sew top edge of tail around tail opening. Join back neck seam for 6¼"/16cm from top of head shaping. Join rem of back seam, leaving an opening at base for stuffing. Stuff toy firmly and close opening. Join arm seams. Join cast-on edge of arms, matching markers. Stuff arms lightly. Sew a tight running st through both thicknesses of arm, between markers at cast-on edge and markers for beg of fingers. Sew running st as before, halfway between first running sts and each edge of hand, forming four fingers. Sew arms to each side of body, placing bound off sts of arms between markers on body. Using satin stitch and stem stitch and B and C, embroider eyes. Secure 6 ends of C with small sts to top of eyes and trim to ³⁄₈"/1cm lengths to form eyelashes. Cut circles from felt and glue to tail, back and neck.

Keep the freezing temperatures at bay with this chill-chasing chum from the Arctic Circle. Two-stranded knitting gives him a sturdy thick coat, but it's the felting that creates his cozy hugability.

due north

materials

Montera by Classic Elite Yarns, 3½oz/100g balls, each approx 128yds/117m (wool/llama)
2 balls #3816 White (A)
LaGran by Classic Elite Yarns, 1½oz/42g balls, each approx 90yds/81m (mohair/wool/nylon)
2 balls #6501 White (B)
One pair size 10 (6mm) needles
OR SIZE TO OBTAIN GAUGE
One set (4) size 10 (6mm) double-pointed needles (dpn)
Small amount black wool or 6-strand floss for embroidery
Small amount of white cotton yarn
Fiberfill
Stitch marker
Yarn needle

FINISHED MEASUREMENTS

12"/30.5cm long x 8½"/21.5cm tall

GAUGE

10 sts and 20 rows to 4"/10cm over garter st using size 10 (6mm) needles and one strand of A and B held tog (before felting).
TAKE TIME TO CHECK YOUR GAUGE.

STITCH GLOSSARY

SWT slip, wrap, turn

KNIT SIDE

Wyib, sl next st purlwise. Move yarn between the needles to the front. Sl the same st back to LH needle. Turn work, bring yarn to the p side between needles. One st is wrapped. When short rows are completed, work to just before wrapped st, insert RH needle under the wrap and knitwise into the wrapped st, k them tog.

Continued on page 88

Designed by Denise Powell

d u e   n o r t h

Continued from page 86

PURL SIDE

Wyif, sl next st purlwise. Move yarn between the needles to the back of work. Sl same st back to LH

needle. Turn work, bring yarn back to the p side between the needles. One st is wrapped. When short rows are completed, work to just before wrapped st, insert RH needle from behind into the back lp of the wrap and place on LH needle; P wrap tog with st on needle.

NOTES

Work with one strand of A and B held tog, unless otherwise stated. Bear body is made in one piece, beg and ending at back seam. Use the knitting-on method whenever directions state to cast on. Tail, ears and toes are made by casting on sts, then binding them off.

BODY

Beg at back edge, with straight needles and A and B held tog, cast on 26 sts.

Upper body *Row 1 and all odd rows to row 17* Knit.

Row 2 K10, [M1, k1] 6 times, M1, k10—33 sts.

Row 4 K10, M1, [k2, M1] 3 times, k1, M1, [k2, M1] 3 times, k10—41 sts.

Row 6 K10, M1, [k3, M1] 7 times, k10—49 sts.

Row 8 K24, cast on 4 sts, bind off 4 sts (tail made), k24.

Row 10 K41, SWT, k33, SWT, k30, SWT, k27, SWT, k24, SWT, k21, SWT, k18, SWT, k15, SWT, k12, SWT, k9, SWT, k29.

Row 12 K4, SWT, k4, turn, k3, SWT, k3, turn, k2, SWT, k2, turn, k39, SWT, k29, SWT, k25, SWT, k21, SWT, k35, turn, k4, SWT, k4, turn, k3, SWT, k3, turn, k2, SWT, k2.

Row 14 K4, SWT, k4, turn, k3, SWT, k3, turn, k2, SWT, k2, turn, k12, SWT, k3, SWT, k4, SWT, k5, SWT, k6, SWT, k7, SWT, k33, SWT, k3, SWT, k4, SWT, k5, SWT, k6, SWT, k7, SWT, k14, turn, k4, SWT, k4, turn, k3, SWT, k3, turn, k2, SWT, k2.

Row 16 Bind off first 10 sts (right rear leg), knit to end—39 sts.

Row 17 Bind off first 10 sts (left rear leg), k to end—29 sts.

Row 18 [K1, M1] twice, k25, [M1, k1] twice—33 sts.

Row 19 and all odd rows to row 27 Knit.

Row 20 [K2, M1] twice, k25, [M1, k2] twice—37 sts.

Row 22 Knit.

Row 24 K1, k2tog, k31, k2tog, k1—35 sts.

Row 26 Cast on 10 sts (right front leg), k10, k1tbl, k to end—45 sts.

Row 27 Cast on 10 sts (left front leg), k10, k1tbl, k to end—55 sts.

Row 28 K37, SWT, k19, SWT, k16, SWT, k13, SWT, k10, SWT, k7, SWT, k31.

Row 29 and all odd rows to row 39 Knit.

Row 30 Knit.

Row 32 K12, SWT, k7, SWT, k8, SWT, k6, SWT, k41, SWT, k6, SWT, k8, SWT, k7, SWT, k12.

Row 34 K4, SWT, k4, turn, k3, SWT, k3, turn, k2, SWT, k2, turn, k 25, M1, k5, M1, k25, turn, k4, SWT, k4, turn, k3, SWT, k3, turn, k2, SWT, k2—57 sts.

Row 36 K4, SWT, k4, turn, k3, SWT, k3, turn, k2, SWT, k2, turn, k 57, turn, k4, SWT, k4, turn, k3, SWT, k3, turn, k2, SWT, k2.

Row 38 Bind off first 10 sts (right front leg), k2tog, k31, k2tog, k to end—45 sts.

Row 39 Bind off first 10 sts (left front leg), k to end—35 sts.

Row 40 [K2tog] twice, k5, [k2tog] twice, k9, [k2tog] twice, k5, [k2tog] twice—27 sts.

Row 41 and all odd rows to row 101 Knit.

Row 42 [K2tog] twice, k19, [k2tog] twice—23 sts.

Row 44 K2tog, k19, k2tog—21 sts.

Row 46 K2tog, k17, k2tog—19 sts.

Row 48 Knit.

Row 50 K2tog, k15, k2tog—17 sts.

Row 52 K5, cast on 3 sts, bind off 3 sts (right ear made), k5, cast on 3 sts, bind off 3 sts (left ear made), k5.

Row 54 K4, k2tog, k5, k2tog, k4—15 sts.

Row 56 Knit.

Row 58 K4, k2tog, k3, k2tog, k4—13 sts.

Row 60 Knit.

Row 62 [K2tog] twice, k5, [k2tog] twice—9 sts.

Row 64 K2tog, k1, sl 2 knitwise, k1, p2sso, k1, k2tog—5 sts.

Rows 66 and 68 Knit.

Row 70 K1, slip 2 knitwise, k1, p2sso, k1—3 sts (tip of nose).

Under body Row 72 [K1, M1] twice, k1—5 sts.

Rows 74 and 76 Knit.

Row 78 K1, M1, k3, M1, k1—7 sts.

Row 80 Knit.

Row 82 K1, M1, k5, M1, k1—9 sts.

Rows 84, 86 and 88 Knit.

Row 90 K1, M1, k7, M1, k1—11 sts.

Rows 92 and 94 Knit.

Row 96 K1, M1, k9, M1, k1—13 sts.

Row 98 Knit.

Row 100 Cast on 8 sts (right front leg) and k8, k1tbl, k1, k2tog, k5, k2tog, k2—19 sts.

Row 101 Cast on 8 sts (left front leg) and k8, k1tbl, k to end—27 sts.

Row 102 K3, SWT, k3, turn, k2, SWT, k2, turn, k10, k2tog, k3, k2tog, k10, turn, k3, SWT, k3, turn, k2, SWT, k2—25 sts.

Continued on page 90

Continued from page 89.

Row 103 and all odd rows to row 111 **Knit.**

Row 104 **K10, k2tog, k1, k2tog, k10—23 sts.**

Row 106 **Knit.**

Row 108 **K10, M1, k3, M1, k10—25 sts.**

Row 110 **Bind off first 9 sts (right front leg), k to end—16 sts.**

Row 111 **Bind off first 9 sts (left front leg), k to end—7 sts.**

Row 112 **[K1, M1] twice, k3, [M1, k1] twice—11 sts.**

Row 113 and all odd rows to row 119 **Knit.**

Row 114 **K8, SWT, k5, SWT, k8.**

Row 116 **K9, SWT, k7, SWT, k5, SWT, k3, SWT, k7.**

Row 118 **Cast on 9 sts (right rear leg), k to end—20 sts.**

Row 119 **Cast on 9 sts (left rear leg), k to end—29 sts.**

Row 120 **K4, SWT, k4, turn, k3, SWT, k3, turn, k2, SWT, k2, turn, k 10, [k2tog] twice, k1, [k2tog] twice, k10, turn, k4, SWT, k4, turn, k3, SWT, k3, turn, k2, SWT, k2—25 sts.**

Row 121 and all odd rows to row 127 **Knit.**

Row 122 **K10, k2tog, k1, k2tog, k10—23 sts.**

Row 124 **K19, SWT, k15, SWT, k13, SWT, k11, SWT, k17.**

Row 126 **K10, M1, k3, M1, k10—25 sts.**

Row 127 **Knit. Bind off.** Using 1 strand of A, sew seams, matching corners of legs and easing upper body neck and head to match lower body. Leave a 3"/7.5cm opening along rear seam for stuffing and leave bottom of legs open.

Rear paws With RS facing, dpn and 2 strands of A held tog, beg at back seam of rear leg and pick and k around bottom edge as foll: 7 sts on first dpn, 9 sts on 2nd dpn, 7 sts on 3rd dpn—23 sts. Join and pm for beg of rnds.

Rnd 1 **P9, [cast on 3 sts, bind off 3 sts] 5 times (toes made), p9.**

Rnd 2 **K1, k2tog, k4, k2tog, k5, k2tog, k4, k2tog, k1—19 sts.**

Rnd 3 **K2tog, k15, k2tog—17 sts.**

Rnd 4 **[K2tog] 3 times, k5, [k2tog] 3 times—11 sts.**

Rnd 5 **K2, k2tog, k3, k2tog, k2—9 sts.**

Rnd 6 **[K2tog] twice, k1, [k2tog] twice—5 sts.** Cut yarn leaving a long tail. Thread tail into tapestry needle and weave through sts. Pull tight to gather; fasten off securely.

Front paws With RS facing, dpn and 2 strands of A held tog, beg at back seam of front leg and pick and k around bottom edge as foll: 7 sts on first dpn, 7 sts on 2nd dpn and 7 sts on 3rd dpn—21 sts. Join and pm for beg of rnds.

Rnd 1 **P8, [cast on 3 sts, bind off 3 sts] 5 times (toes made), p8.**

Rnd 2 **K2tog, k4, k2tog, k5, k2tog, k4, k2tog—17 sts.**

Rnd 3 **K2tog, k13, k2tog—15 sts.**

Rnd 4 **[K2tog] 3 times, k3, [k2tog] 3 times—9 sts.** *Rnd 5* **K2tog, k5, k2tog—7 sts.** Cut yarn leaving a long tail. Thread tail into tapestry needle and weave through sts. Pull tight to gather. Fasten off securely.

Felting Lightly stuff body, head and legs with plastic bags. Whip-stitch opening closed, temporarily, using cotton yarn. Place bear in a mesh bag (it will shed while being felted). Machine-wash in hot water, then rinse with cold water. It may take two washings before felting is achieved. Remove cotton yarn stitching and plastic bags. Let bear dry completely.

Embroidery Stuff head with fiberfill. Thread black wool or six-strand floss into tapestry needle and knot end. Working from inside of head, insert needle so it exits at position of first eye. Make a small st, then insert needle through head so it exits at position of second eye. Pull tightly to form indents for eyes, then make another small stitch to secure. Working in satin stitch, embroider this eye, then insert needle through head so it exits at position of first eye and embroider that eye. Insert needle through head so it exits at position of nose; do not pull tight. Embroider a satin-stitch nose and straight stitch mouth. Insert needle back into head and fasten off securely. Stuff rem body and legs. Using 1 strand of A, sew opening closed.

You don't have to walk on pins and needles around this porcupine!
His graceful snout and chubby body are almost effortless to make in imitation fur yarn
and gray wool blend, with an easy cherry nose topping things off.

the whole (hedge)hog

materials
Wool Ease by Lion Brand Yarns,
3oz/85g balls, each approx
197yds/177m (acrylic/wool)
1 skein in #403 Mushroom Heather (A)
*Small amounts each of
#139 Dark Rose Heather (C) and
#179 Chestnut Heather (D)
for embroidering eyes and snout
Fun Fur by Lion Brand Yarns
1³⁄₄oz/50g balls, each approx
60yds/54m (polyester)
1 skein in #204 Lava (B)
One pair size 7 (4.5mm) needles
OR SIZE TO OBTAIN GAUGE
Fiberfill
Yarn needle
1 square of Taupe felt

Designed by Amy Bahrt

FINISHED MEASUREMENTS

6½"/16.5cm long

GAUGE

18 sts and 24 rows to 4"/10cm over St st with A using size 7 (4.5mm) needles. TAKE TIME TO CHECK YOUR GAUGE.

HEAD

With A, cast on 21 sts. Beg with a RS row, work in St st, dec 1 st each side on 3rd row, then every other row 8 times more—3 sts. Work 1 row even. Cut yarn, draw end through rem sts and pull tog tightly. Sew side seam.

BASE

With A, cast on 7 sts. Beg with a RS row, work in St st for 5 rows, inc 1 st each side on rows 3 and 5—11 sts. Work 18 rows even. Bind off.

BACK

With B, cast on 21 sts. Work 20 rows in garter st. Bind off.

FINISHING

Sew back to base (forming a tube), leaving an opening for the head and along the curved portion of the base. Attach head to body, with seam at bottom. Insert stuffing into entire piece. Sew back opening closed. Cut 4 feet from felt, using template. Using matching thread, sew feet to base (2 in front and 2 in back), leaving toes free. With C, work a French knot at tip of snout for nose; with D, work 2 knots for eyes.

template for foot

This pensive bouclé bruin continues a timeless tradition among stuffed animals. With his slightly somber expression and slouchy ribbed sweater, who wouldn't want to give him a heartfelt squeeze?

bear necessity

GAUGE

20 sts and 32 rows to 4"/10cm over St st using size 4 (3.5mm) needles and Wildflower DK.

TAKE TIME TO CHECK YOUR GAUGE.

HEAD

Side Cast on 12 sts. K 2 rows, p 1 row on WS. Cont in St st, inc 1 st at beg of next row (side edge) and cont to inc 1 st at side edge every other row twice more—15 sts. Work even until there are 13 rows from beg.

Next row (RS) Bind off 7 sts, work to end. Work 1 row even. Dec 1 st each side on next row. Work 1 row even.

Next row Dec 1 st, work to end. Work 1 row even. Rep last 2 rows once more. Bind off rem 4 sts. Work 2nd side to correspond, reversing shaping.

Back Cast on 12 sts and k 2 rows. P 1 row on WS.

Next row (RS) [K3, inc 1 st in next st] twice, k to end—14 sts. Work 3 rows even.

Next row [K4, inc 1 st in next st] twice, k to end—16 sts. Work 5 rows even. Dec 1 st each side on next row, then every other row twice more—10 sts. Bind off 2 sts at beg of next 2 rows. Bind off rem 6 sts.

Continued on page 96

materials for bear
Alpaca Bouclé by Plymouth Yarns, 1³/₄/50g balls, each approx 70yds/63m (alpaca/nylon)
2 balls in #11 Tan
Small amount of Brown for embroidery
One pair size 7 (4.5mm) needles
OR SIZE TO OBTAIN GAUGE
Stitch holders
Fiberfill
Yarn needle

materials for sweater
Wildflower DK by Plymouth Yarns, 1³/₄oz/50g balls, each approx 137yds/123m (cotton/acrylic)
1 ball in #40 Off White
Two buttons
One pair size 4 (3.5mm) needles
OR SIZE TO OBTAIN GAUGE
Yarn needle

Diagram 1

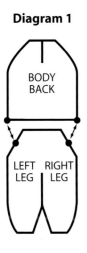

Diagram 2

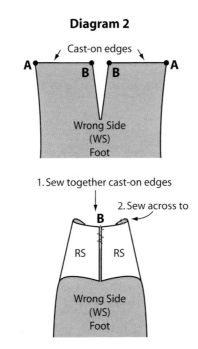

Center Cast on 4 sts. Work in St st, inc 1 st each side on rows 5, 11, 15 and 17. Work even until there are 22 rows from beg. Bind off rem 12 sts.

Base of nose/chin Cast on 2 sts and work in St st, inc 1 st each side every other row 4 times—10 sts. Bind off 3 sts at beg of next 2 rows. Bind off rem 4 sts. Sew sides of head to back head. Sew base of nose/chin to center piece. Sew center piece between side pieces. Stuff head and embroider nose and eyes foll photo.

EARS (MAKE 2)

Cast on 10 sts and work in St st for 4 rows. Dec 1 st each side on next row, then every other row once more. Inc 1 st each side on next RS row then every other row once more. Work 3 rows even. Bind off rem 10 sts. With WS tog, fold in half and sew. Sew to top of head.

BACK BODY

Cast on 26 sts for underside and work in St st for 17 rows.

Next row (WS) Work 13 sts, join 2nd ball of yarn and work to end. Working both sides at once with separate balls, work 1 row even.

Dec row 1 (WS) P2tog, work to end of first half; on 2nd half work to last 2 sts, p2tog. Work 3 rows even.

Dec row 2 P2tog, work to last 2 sts of first half, p2tog; work 2nd half as for first half. Work 1 row even. Rep dec row 1. Work 3 rows even. Work dec row 2. Work 1 row even. Work dec row 1. Work 1 row even. Bind off rem 6 sts each side.

BOTTOM LEG

Cast on 6 sts and work in St st, inc 1 st each side every other row once, every 4th row twice—12 sts. Work even until piece 39 rows have been worked from beg. Place sts on a holder. Make a 2nd piece in same way. Join both pieces and work on 24 sts, dec 1 st each side every other row 5 times. Bind off rem 14 sts. Sew center seam of back body. Sew cast-on edge of back body to bound-off of bottom leg, foll diagram 1.

ARMS (MAKE 2)

Cast on 5 sts for shoulder edge and work in St st for 1 row. Cast on 2 sts at beg of next 2 rows. Inc 1 st each side every other row 5 times—19 sts. Work 13 rows even. Dec 1 st each side every other row 3 times, every 4th row once— 11 sts. Work 1 row even. Bind off. Sew seams and stuff.

Continued on page 98

bear necessity

Continued from page 97

FRONT BODY

Cast on 6 sts for underside of foot and work in St st for 11 rows. Place sts on a holder. Make a 2nd piece in same way. Join both pieces and work on 12 sts for 30 rows. Place sts on a holder. Make a 2nd piece in same way. Join both pieces on one needle—24 sts. Work even for 18 rows. Divide work in half and work as foll: Work 1 row even. Work dec row 2. Work 3 rows even. Work dec row 1. Work 3 rows even. Work dec row 2. Work 3 rows even. Work dec row 1. Work 1 row even. Bind off rem 6 sts each side. Sew center seam. Sew foot foll diagram 2.

FINISHING

Sew front to back and stuff. Sew on head. Sew on arms.

SWEATER

Back Cast on 44 sts and work in rib as foll:
Row 1 (RS) P3, *k2, p2; rep from *, end last rep p3 instead of 2.
Row 2 K the knit sts and p the purl sts. Cont in rib as established until piece measures 6"/15cm from beg.
Shoulder shaping Bind off 12 sts at beg of next 2 rows. Bind off rem 20 sts for back neck.
Front Work as for back until piece measures 2¾"/7cm from beg.
Placket shaping
Next row (RS) Work 21 sts, inc 1 st in next st, join 2nd ball of yarn, inc 1 st in next st, work to end. Work both sides at once with separate balls of yarn and keep 2 sts at neck edge in garter st and rem sts in rib until same length as back to shoulder. Shape shoulder as for back. Bind off

rem11 sts each side for neck.
Sleeves Cast on 23 sts and work in rib as for back until piece measures 2¼"/5.5cm. Bind off.

FINISHING

Block pieces. Sew shoulder seams. With center of top of sleeve at shoulder seam, sew sleeve to front and back. Sew side and sleeve seams. Make two chain button loops on one side of placket. Sew buttons to other side of placket.

A baby's first toy should be soothing, gentle, and most importantly, washable.
Created with mild, terry-inspired yarn in relaxing yellow and blue,
this blooming flower figure definitely fits the bill.

o o p s y d a i s y

materials

Polarspun by Lion Brand Yarns,
1¾oz/50g balls, each approx
137yds/123m (polyester)
2 balls in #157 Polar Yellow (MC)
Baby Soft by Lion Brand Yarns,
5oz/140g balls, each approx
459yds/413m (acrylic/nylon)
small amounts each of
#100 White (A), #157 Pastel Yellow (B)
and #156 Pastel Green (C)
1yd/1m each of Dark Brown yarn
(for embroidering face)
Black yarn (for eyelashes) and
Light Brown yarn (for hair)
One pair each sizes 6 and 9
(4 and 5.5mm) needles
OR SIZE TO OBTAIN GAUGE
Fiberfill
Yarn needle

FINISHED MEASUREMENTS

19"/48cm long

GAUGE

13 sts and 20 rows to 4"/10cm over St st with MC using larger needles.

TAKE TIME TO CHECK YOUR GAUGE.

BODY BACK

Foot With smaller needles and A, cast on 4 sts.

Row 1 (RS) Knit.

Row 2 P1, M1, p to last st, M1, p1.

Row 3 K1, M1, k to last st, M1, k1. Rep rows 2 and 3 once more, then row 2 once more—14 sts. Work 6 rows even in St st. Change to larger needles and MC.

Shape leg *Row 1 (RS)* K1, [k2tog] 6 times, k1—8 sts.

Row 2 Purl.

Row 3 [K2, M1] 3 times, k2—11 sts.

Row 4 Purl.

Row 5 [K1, M1] 9 times, k2—20 sts. Work 13 rows even. Break MC. Slide sts over

Continued on page 102

Designed by Gayle Bunn

o o p s y   d a i s y

Continued from page 101

and, with A, cast on 4 sts onto end of same needle. Make 2nd leg in same manner. Do not break MC.

Join legs *Row 1 (RS)* K20 from 2nd leg, then k20 from first leg—40 sts. Work 5 rows even. Dec 1 st each side on next row, then every 4th row twice more—34 sts. Work 3 rows even.

Next row (RS) [K2tog] 17 times—17 sts.

Next row Purl.

Shape arms Cast on 3 sts at beg of next 4 rows—29 sts. Work 8 rows even. Bind off 5 sts at beg of next 4 rows. Bind off rem 9 sts.

Hand With RS facing, smaller needles and A, pick up and k 11 sts along end of each arm. Beg with a p row, work 7 rows in St st. Cont in St st, dec 1 st each side of next 4 rows—3 sts.

Next row (RS) SK2P. Fasten off last st.

BODY FRONT

Work as for body back.

Face With smaller needles and A, cast on 15 sts. Work 2 rows in St st. Inc 1 st each side on next row, then every other row 7 times more—31 sts. Work 5 rows even. Dec 1 st each side on next row, then every other row 7 times more—15 sts. P 1 row. Bind off.

Back of head With larger needles and MC, cast on 9 sts. Work 2 rows in St st. Inc 1 st each side on next row, then every other row 4 times more—19 sts. Work 3 rows even. Dec 1 st each side on next row, then every other row 4 times more—9 sts. P 1 row. Bind off.

Solid petal (make 4) With larger needles and MC, cast on 9 sts. Work 8 rows in St st. Dec 1 st each side on next row, then every other row twice more—3 sts.

Next row (WS) Purl. Inc 1 st each side on next row, then every other row twice more—9 sts. Work 9 rows even. Bind off. Fold petal in half and sew side edges tog.

Gingham petal front (make 3) With smaller needles and B, cast on 16 sts. Work 15 rows of Chart. Bind off rem 2 sts.

Gingham petal back (make 3) With larger needles and MC, cast on 9 sts. Work 8 rows in St st. Dec 1 st each side on next row, then every other row twice more—3 sts. P 1 row.

Next row SK2P. Fasten off last st. Sew Gingham Petal Front to Gingham Petal Back.

FINISHING

Sew body front and back tog, leaving an opening at neck and one inner leg to insert stuffing. Stuff feet and hands firmly. Stuff remainder of body lightly. With A, stitch across ends of feet and hands to enclose stuffing. Sew leg opening closed. Sew face to back of head, leaving neck open. Stuff head. Sew head to neck. Embroider face details, using photo as guide. With light brown yarn, make 3 short twisted cords for hair and sew in position at top of face. With 4 strands of B held tog, make twisted cord long enough to fit around face with a 5"/12.5cm extension at each side for bow under chin. Sew cord in position and tie bow. Sew petals around head, alternating gingham and solid petals.

Chart

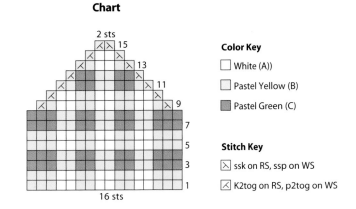

Color Key

☐ White (A))

☐ Pastel Yellow (B)

■ Pastel Green (C)

Stitch Key

⋋ ssk on RS, ssp on WS

⋌ K2tog on RS, p2tog on WS

Whether it's naptime or playtime, this panda rug is the ideal accessory.
His hefty body is worked in one piece for easy finishing, and a chunky layer of fiberfill
makes him a snuggly spot for a comfortable afternoon snooze.

wild by design

materials
Plush by Berroco, Inc., 1¾oz/50g balls,
each approx 90yds/83m
(cotton/acrylic)
8 balls in #18 White (A)
7 balls in #26 Black (B)
One pair size 10 (6mm) needles,
OR SIZE TO OBTAIN GAUGE
Size 10 (6mm) circular needle,
40"/100cm long
One set (4) size 10 (6mm) double-
pointed needles (dpn)
Stitch marker and holders
36" x 36" (92cm x 92cm)
Fiberfill
One square each of white
and pink felt
Fabric glue
Felt tip marker
Yarn needle

FINISHED MEASUREMENTS

Height (from top of head to tip of paws) 32"/81cm

Width 22"/56cm

GAUGE

12 sts and 20 rows to 4"/10cm over St st using size 10 (6mm) needles and 2 strands of yarn held tog. TAKE TIME TO CHECK YOUR GAUGE.

NOTE

Entire bear is worked with 2 strands of yarn held tog throughout.

BODY

With circular needle and 2 strands A, cast on 126 sts, placing markers on cast-on edge as foll: 18 sts, place marker (pm), 27 sts, pm, 36 sts, 27 sts, pm, 18 sts, pm for end of rnd (sl this marker every rnd). Join, and work in St st (k every rnd) for 8"/20.5cm. Break A. Join B and work 14"/35.5cm more in St st, ending last rnd 16 sts before rnd marker. Piece measures 22"/56cm from beg. Do not cut yarn. Set aside.

Continued on page 106

Designed by Jean Guirguis

wild by design

Continued from page 104

HEAD

(*Note* Work entire head using straight needles and 2 strands A.)

Right side Cast on 15 sts. K 2 rows. P 1 row on WS. Cont in St st, inc 1 st at side edge (beg of RS rows) on next row, then every other row twice more—18 sts. Work 7 rows even.

Next row (RS) Bind off 7 sts, k to end. Work 1 row even. Dec 1 st each side on next row. Work 1 row even. *

Next row (RS) Dec 1 st, k to end. Work 1 row even. Rep from * once more. Bind off rem 7 sts.

Left side Work to correspond to right side, reversing shaping by working side edge incs and decs at end of RS rows. Bind off at beg of a WS row.

Back Cast on 15 sts. K 2 rows. P 1 row on WS.

Next row (RS) K4, inc 1 st in next st, k5, inc 1 st in next st, k4—17 sts. Work 5 rows even.

Next row (RS) [K5, inc 1 st in next st] twice, k5—19 sts. Work 5 rows even. Dec 1 st each side on next row, then every other row twice more—13 sts. Work 1 row even. Bind off 2 sts at beg of next 2 rows. Bind off rem 9 sts.

Front Cast on 7 sts. Work in St st, inc 1 st each side on rows 5, 11, 15 and 17. Work 5 rows even. Bind off 15 sts.

Base of nose/chin Cast on 3 sts. Work in St st, inc 1 st each side on 3rd row, then every other row 4 times more—13 sts. Work 1 row even. Bind off 3 sts at beg of next 2 rows. Bind off rem 7 sts. Sew sides of head to back. Sew base of nose/chin to cast-on sts of front. Sew front and nose/chin piece between side pieces.

Underside of head With RS facing and A, pick up and k12 sts along cast-on edge of chin. Work in St st, pick up one st from edge on each side until there are 24 sts. Dec 1 st each side every row 7 times—10 sts. Bind off.

Stuff head. Sew seam along bottom of head, sewing back and front tog.

EARS (MAKE 2)

With B, cast on 12 sts. Work in St st for 8 rows. Dec 1 st each side on next row. Work 1 row even. Rep last 2 rows once more—8 sts. Inc 1 st each side on next row. Work 1 row even. Rep last 2 rows once more—12 sts. Work 7 rows even. Bind off. Fold ear in half and sew side seams. Sew ears to top of head.

Right Eye With B, cast on 2 sts. Work in St st, inc 1 st at end of every RS row 4 times—6 sts. Work 1 row even.

Next row (RS) Ssk, k to end.

Next row P to last 2 sts, ssp.

Next row Ssk, k2tog. P 1 row. Bind off.

Left eye With B, cast on 2 sts. Work in St st, inc 1 st at beg of every RS row 4 times—6 sts. Work 1 row even.

Paw Template

Next row (RS) K to last 2 sts, k2tog.

Next row P2tog, p to end.

Next row Ssk, k2tog. P 1 row. Bind off. Sew eyes in place. With 1 strand B, embroider nose and mouth, using photo as guide. Return to body sts on circular needle.

Next rnd K32 (for front paw), bind off next 31 sts, k until there are 32 sts on needle (for 2nd paw) and place these sts on a holder, bind off 31 sts.

FRONT PAWS

Work 32 sts as foll: with first dpn, k16, with 2nd dpn, k8, with 3rd dpn, k8. Work 4"/10cm in St st.

Dec rnd (Needle 1) K1, ssk, k to last 3 sts, k2tog, k1; (Needle 2) K1, ssk, k to end; (Needle 3) K to last 3 sts, k2tog, k1.

Next rnd Knit. Rep last 2 rnds 3 times more—16 sts. Sl sts from 2nd dpn onto 3rd dpn and graft sts tog, using Kitchener st. Join yarn to 32 sts on other side and work 2nd front paw as for first. Sew center 31 sts of back to 31 sts of front. Sew on head, centered between paws.

BACK PAWS

With RS facing, dpns and B, pick up and k36 sts between markers along cast-on edge of body as foll: 18 sts on first needle, and 9 sts on each of the other 2 needles. Work in St st for 4"/10cm. Work Dec rnds as for front paws until there are 16 sts. Complete as for front paws. Pick up sts for other paw between markers on other side and work as for first paw.

TAIL

With A, cast on 16 sts. Work in St st for 3½"/9cm, end with a WS row. Dec 1 st each side every RS row 3 times—10 sts. Bind off. Fold both sides of cast-on edge to WS so that edges meet in center. Sew cast-on edge to back of body, approx 3"/7.5cm up from cast-on edge.

FINISHING

Place bear on flat piece of fiberfill and trace shape of body and paws with felt tip marker. Cut out shape and stuff into bear, making sure fiberfill is not twisted. Sew bottom seam between paws. Cut paw prints from pink felt, using templates, and glue to bottom of back paws. Cut crescent shapes from white felt and glue to eyes. With A, embroider claws on front paws.

It doesn't matter if she's going to the market or rolling in mud on the farm as long as this pastel piggy eventually comes all the way home. She's a cinch to knit in cotton candy pink, accented with lively country checks and a darling corkscrew tail.

p i g t a l e

Designed by Gayle Bunn

materials
Polarspun by Lion Brand Yarns,
1¾oz/50g balls, each approx
137yds/123m (polyester)
1 ball in #101 Polar Pink (MC)
Baby Soft by Lion Brand Yarns,
5oz/140g balls, each approx
459yds/413m acrylic, nylon)
small amounts each of
#101 Pastel Pink (A),
#100 White (B), and #103 Bubble Gum (C)
1yd/1m of dark brown yarn for
embroidering eyes and snout
One pair each sizes 6 and 9
(4 and 5.5mm) needles
OR SIZE TO OBTAIN GAUGE
Stitch markers
Fiberfill
Yarn needle

FINISHED MEASUREMENTS

11"/28cm long

GAUGE

13 sts and 20 rows to 4"/10cm over St st with MC using larger needles.

TAKE TIME TO CHECK YOUR GAUGE.

UPPER BODY

With larger needles and MC, cast on 48 sts, placing a marker after first 9 sts and before last 9 sts. Work 10 rows in St st.

Shape back legs Bind off 4 sts at beg of next 2 rows. Dec 1 st each side of next 5 rows—30 sts. Work 9 rows even.

Shape front legs *Inc row (RS)* K1, M1, k to last st, M1, k1. Work 1 row even. Rep last 2 rows 3 times more—38 sts.

Next row (RS) K1, M1, k12, bind off next 12 sts, k to last st, M1, k1. Cont on last 14 sts only.

Left leg *Next row (WS)* Purl. Dec 1 st each side on next row, then every other row 5 times more—2 sts. Work 1 row even. Bind off.

Right leg With WS facing, join yarn and work as for left leg.

Continued on page 110

pig tale

Continued from page 108

GUSSET AND LOWER BODY

With larger needles and MC, cast on 3 sts. Work 2 rows in St st.

Inc row (RS) K1, M1, k to last st, M1, k1. Work 3 rows even. Rep last 4 rows 4 times more—13 sts. Work 4 more rows even in St st. Place markers each side of row.

Shape back legs Cast on 9 sts at beg of next 2 rows—31 sts. Work 10 rows even. Bind off 4 sts at beg of next 2 rows. Dec 1 st each side of next 5 rows—13 sts. Work 9 rows even.

Shape front legs *Row 1 (RS)* K1, M1, k5, M1, k1, M1, k5, M1, k1—17 sts.

Rows 2, 4 and 6 Purl.

Row 3 K1, M1, k7, M1, k1, M1, k7, M1, k1—21 sts.

Row 5 K1, M1, k9, M1, k1, M1, k9, M1, k1—25 sts.

Row 7 K12, M1, k1, M1, k12—27 sts.

Row 8 Purl.

Next row (RS) K1, M1, k12, bind off center st, k to last st, M1, k1. Cont on last 14 sts only.

Right leg *Next row (WS)* Purl. Dec 1 st each side on next row, then every other row 5 times more—2 sts. Work 1 row even. Bind off.

Left leg With WS facing, join yarn and work as for right leg.

HEAD

With larger needles and 2 strands of MC held tog, cast on 7 sts. P 1 row on WS.

Next row (RS) K1, [M1, k1] 6 times—13 sts. Work 1 row even.

Next row K1, [M1, k1] 12 times—25 sts. Work 3 rows even.

Next row K2, [M1, k3] 7 times, M1, k2—33 sts. Work 13 rows even.

Shape snout *Next row (RS)* K1, [k2tog] 16 times—17 sts. Work 3 rows even. Bind off. Fold in half and sew seam. Insert stuffing through snout opening.

Outer ears (Make 2) With larger needles and MC, cast on 11 sts. K 7 rows.

Next row (RS) K1, ssk, k to last 3 sts, k2tog, k1.

Next row Knit. Rep last 2 rows twice more—5 sts.

Next row (RS) Ssk, k1, k2tog.

Next row K3.

Next row SK2P. Fasten off.

Inner ears (make 2) With smaller needles and A, cast on 16 sts. Work 15 rows of Chart 1. Bind off rem 2 sts.

BACK FEET PADS AND SNOUT

With smaller needles and A, cast on 4 sts. Work 12 rows of Chart 2. Bind off rem 4 sts.

FRONT FEET PADS

With smaller needles and A, cast on 6 sts. Work 15 rows of Chart 3. Bind off rem 6 sts.

FINISHING

Sew inner ear to outer ear. Sew lower body to upper body, matching markers at back. Leave feet open. Leave an opening at neck and back to insert stuffing. Stuff body firmly. Sew feet pads in position. Sew openings closed. Sew head to neck. Sew ears to head. Embroider face details, using photo as a guide.

TAIL

With 2 strands each of MC and A, make a twisted cord 3½"/9cm long and attach to back of body.

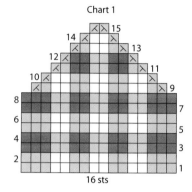

Chart 1

16 sts

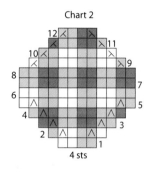

Chart 2

4 sts

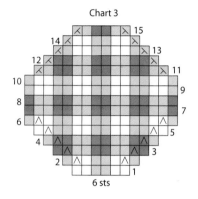

Chart 3

6 sts

Color Key

- Pastel pink (A)
- White (B)
- Bubble gum (C)

Stitch Key

- ⟋ Ssk on RS, Ssp on WS
- ⟍ K2 tog on RS, p2 tog on WS
- ⋀ Make 1 (M1)

Droopy ears and a preppy pullover make man's best friend stylish
as well as squeezable. Perk up his eyes and nose with chunky yarn and velvet,
and celebrate his cherished snack with a felt bone decal.

preppy pup

FINISHED MEASUREMENTS

Chest 20"/51cm

Length 21"/53.5cm

GAUGE

14 sts and 22 rows to 4"/10cm over St st using size 10 (6mm) needles.

TAKE TIME TO CHECK YOUR GAUGE.

HEAD

Right side Cast on 12 sts. K 2 rows. P 1 row on WS. Cont in St st, inc 1 st at side edge (beg of RS rows) on next row, then every other row twice more—15 sts. Work 5 rows even.

Next row (RS) Bind off 7 sts, k to end. Work 1 row even. Dec 1 st each side on next row. Work 1 row even.

*Next row (RS) Dec 1 st, k to end. Work 1 row even. Rep from * once more. Bind off rem 4 sts.

Left side Work to correspond to right side, reversing shaping by working side edge incs and decs at end of RS rows. Bind off at beg of a WS row.

Back Cast on 12 sts. K 2 rows. P 1 row on WS.

Next row (RS) K3, inc 1 st in next st, k4, inc 1 st in next st, k3—14 sts. Work 3 rows even.

Continued on page 114

materials for dog

Zucca by Trendsetter Yarns, 1³⁄₄oz/50g balls, each approx 71yds/64m (tactel/polyamid)

4 balls in #5536 Brown

Small amount each of bulky black and white yarn for embroidering eyes and mouth

One pair size 10 (6mm) needles

OR SIZE TO OBTAIN GAUGE

Stitch holders

Fiberfill

One black velvet button (for nose)

Yarn needle

materials for sweater

Provence by Classic Elite Yarns, 4oz/125g balls, each approx 256yds/236m (cotton)

1 hank in #2608 Blue

One pair size 6 (4mm) needles

Piece of white felt for bone appliqué

Fabric glue

Yarn needle

Designed by Jean Guirguis

preppy pup

Continued from page 113

Next row (RS) [K4, inc 1 st in next st] twice, k4—16 sts. Work 5 rows even. Dec 1 st each side on next row, then every other row twice more—10 sts. Work 1 row even. Bind off 2 sts at beg of next 2 rows. Bind off rem 6 sts.

Front Cast on 4 sts. Work in St st, inc 1 st each side on rows 5, 11, 15 and 17. Work 5 rows even. Bind off 12 sts.

Base of nose/chin Cast on 2 sts. Work in St st, inc 1 st each side on 3rd row, then every other row 3 times more—10 sts. Work 1 row even. Bind off 3 sts at beg of next 2 rows. Bind off rem 4 sts. Sew sides of head to back. Sew base of nose/chin to cast-on sts of front. Sew front and nose/chin piece between side pieces. Stuff

head and embroider eyes with French knots. Sew on button for nose. Embroider mouth under nose.

EARS (MAKE 2)

Pick up and k10 sts on top of head and work in St st for 8"/20.5cm. Bind off.

BODY BACK

Cast on 26 sts and work in St st for 19 rows.
Dec Row 1 (WS) P2tog, p last 2 sts, p2tog. Work 3 rows even.
Dec Row 2 P2tog, p8, [p2tog] twice, p to last 2 sts, p2tog. Work 1 row even. Work Dec Row 1. Work 1 row even.
Dec Row 3 P2tog, p5, [p2tog] twice, p to last 2 sts, p2tog. Work 1 row even. Work Dec Row 1. Work 1 row even. Bind off rem 12 sts.

RIGHT LEG

Cast on 6 sts and work in St st, inc 1 st each side on 3rd row, then every 4th row twice more—12 sts. Work 28 rows even. Break yarn. Place sts on a holder.

LEFT LEG

Work as for right leg, but do not break yarn.
Join legs *Next row (WS)* P across 12 sts of each leg—24 sts. Cont in St st, dec 1 st each side

every RS row 5 times—14 sts. Work 1 row even. Bind off. Sew center seam of body back. Sew cast-on edge of body back to bound-off edge and 5 dec sts each side of back legs foll Diagram 1.

ARMS (MAKE 2)

Cast on 5 sts (shoulder edge). K 1 row. Cont in St st, cast on 2 sts at beg of next 2 rows. Inc 1 st each side every RS row 5 times—19 sts. Work 13 rows even. Dec 1 st each side every RS row 3 times, then every 4th row once—11 sts. Work 1 row even. Bind off. Sew seams and stuff arms.

BODY FRONT

Left leg Cast on 6 sts (underside of foot) and work in St st for 11 rows. Break yarn. Place sts on a holder. Make a 2nd piece in same way, but do not break yarn.

Join pieces *Next row (WS)* P across 6 sts of each piece—12 sts. Cont in St st for 28 rows more. Break yarn. Place sts on a holder.

Right leg Work as for left leg, but do not break yarn.

Join legs *Next row (WS)* P across 12 sts of each leg—24 sts. Work 18 rows even. Divide work.

Next row (RS) K12, join 2nd ball of yarn and k12. Working both sides at once, work as foll: Work Dec Row 2 (as for body back), work 3 rows even, work Dec Row 1, work 3 rows even, work Dec Row 2, work 3 rows even, work Dec Row 1, work 1 row even. Bind off rem 6 sts each side. Sew center seam. Sew feet foll Diagram 2.

FINISHING

Sew body front to back tog, leaving an opening for the arms and stuff. Sew on head. Sew on arms.

SWEATER

FINISHED MEASUREMENTS

Chest 20"/51cm

Length 6¾"/17cm

GAUGE

19 sts and 28 rows to 4"/10 cm over St st using size 6 (4mm) needles.

TAKE TIME TO CHECK YOUR GAUGE.

SEED ST

Row 1 *K1, p1; rep from*, end k1.

Row 2 K the purl sts and p the knit sts. Rep row 2 for seed st.

Back Cast on 47 sts. Work in seed st for ¾"/2cm. Work in St st until piece measures 6¾"/17cm from beg. Bind off.

Front Work as for back until piece measures 5¾"/14.5cm from beg, end with a WS row.

Shape neck *Next row (RS)* K18, join 2nd ball of yarn and bind off center 11 sts, k to end. Working both sides at once, bind off from each neck edge 2 sts once. Dec 1 st each side every RS row twice—14 sts each side. Work 1 row even. Bind off.

SLEEVES

Cast on 33 sts. Work in seed st for ¾"/2cm. Work in St st until piece measures 4¾"/12cm from beg. Bind off.

FINISHING

Block pieces. Sew one shoulder seam.

Neckband With RS facing, pick up and k 39 sts evenly around neck edge. Work 3 rows in Seed St. Bind off. Sew rem shoulder seam, including neckband. With center of top of sleeve at shoulder seam, sew sleeves to front and back. Sew side and sleeve seams. Cut bone shape out of felt, using template, and affix to front of sweater with glue.

Diagram 1

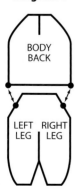

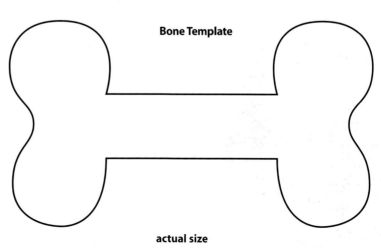

Bone Template

actual size

Make storytelling more exciting with these spirited puppets in irresistible colors. Wide mouths, mischievous eyes and funky details make them totally adorable, not to mention fun!

hand to mouth

FINISHED MEASUREMENTS

Circumference 10½"/27cm

GAUGE

20 sts and 28 rows to 4"/10cm over St st using size 8 (5mm) needles.

TAKE TIME TO CHECK YOUR GAUGE

STITCH GLOSSARY

W&T (wrap and turn)

Short row wrapping *Knit side*

1 Wyib, sl next st purlwise.

2 Move yarn between the needles to the front.

3 Sl the same st back to LH needle. Turn work, bring yarn to the p side between needles. One st is wrapped. When short rows are completed, work to just before wrapped st, insert RH needle under the wrap and

Continued on page 118

materials for big mouth puppet
Cascade 220 by Cascade Yarns,
3½oz/100g balls, each approx
220yds/203m (wool)
1 skein each in #8887 Purple or
#7814 Green (MC), #8895 Red (A),
#7828 Yellow (B)
small amount of orange for hair
One pair size 8 (5mm) needles
OR SIZE TO OBTAIN GAUGE
Yarn needle
2 beads, buttons, or
Wiggle eyes for eyes
One spare needle for working tucks

materials for dragon puppet
Cable needle (cn)
Small amount of tissue or
fiberfill (optional)

Designed by Susan Guagliumi

hand to mouth

Continued from page 117

knitwise into the wrapped st, k them tog.

Purl side

1 Wyif, sl next st purlwise.

2 Move yarn between the needles to the back of work.

3 Sl same st back to LH needle. Turn work, bring yarn back to the p side between the needles. One st is wrapped. When short rows are completed, work to just before wrapped st, insert RH needle from behind into the back lp of the wrap and place on LH needle; P wrap tog with st on needle.

BIG MOUTH PUPPET

BODY FRONT

With MC, cast on 28 sts. Work in k1, p1 rib for 1"/2.5cm. Work in St st until piece measures 7"/18cm from beg, end with a WS row.

Lower Head shaping ***Row 1 (RS)* K27, W&T.

Row 2 P26, W&T.

Row 3 K25, W&T.

Row 4 P24, W&T.

Row 5 K23, W&T.

Row 6 P22, W&T. Cont to work 1 less st before W&T every row until last row worked is: P6, W&T. Break yarn.

Lower Lip *Next row (RS)* Sl all 11 sts from RH needle to LH needle, join A and k28. [P 1 row, k 1 row] 3 times. Work Tuck St:

Next row (WS) Sl tops of MC loops from last MC row worked onto spare needle with tip of needle facing same direction as needle with sts (make sure you have 28 MC sts). Hold needles tog and with A, *p1 st from back needle tog with 1 st from front needle; rep from *. Break yarn.**

Bottom Inside of Mouth *Row 1 (RS)* Sl first 11 sts to RH needle, then join B and K6 center sts, W&T.

Row 2 P7, W&T.

Row 3 K8, W&T.

Row 4 P9, W&T. Cont to work 1 more st before

W&T every row until last row worked is: K26, W&T.

Next row (WS) P27.

Next row K28.

Next row P28.

Upper Inside of Mouth and Upper Lip Rep from ** to ** once.

Upper Head shaping *Row 1 (RS)* Sl first 11 sts to RH needle, then join MC and K6 center sts, W&T.

Row 2 P7, W&T.

Row 3 K8, W&T.

Row 4 P9, W&T. Cont to work 1 more st before W&T every row until last row worked is: K26, W&T.

Next row (WS) P27.

Next row K28.

Next row P28.

BODY BACK

Work even until back measures same length as

Continued on page 120

hand to mouth

Continued from page 118

body front, ending with 1"/2.5cm in k1, p1 rib. Bind off loosely.

FINISHING

Sew side seams.

TONGUE

With A, pick up and k 6 sts along center of inside of mouth and work in garter st for 1"/2.5cm. Dec 1 st each side on next row. Work even for ½"/1.25cm more. Dec 1 st each side on next row. Work even for 1"/2.5cm. Bind off 2 sts. Sew on eyes. Knot strands of C to top of head for hair.

DRAGON PUPPET

BODY FRONT

With MC, cast on 28 sts. Work in k1, p1 rib for 1"/2.5cm. Work in St st until piece measures 7"/18cm from beg, end with a WS row.

Lower Head shaping ***Row 1 (RS)* K27, W&T.

Row 2 P26, W&T.

Row 3 K25, W&T.

Row 4 P24, W&T.

Row 5 K23, W&T.

Row 6 P22, W&T. Cont to work 1 less st before W&T every row until last row worked is: P6, W&T. Break yarn.

Lower Lip *Next row (RS)* Sl all 11 sts from RH needle to LH needle, join A and k28. [P 1 row, k 1 row] 3 times. Work Tuck St:

Next row (WS) Sl tops of MC loops from last MC row worked onto spare needle with tip of needle facing same direction as needle with sts (make sure you have 28 MC sts). Hold needles tog and with A, *p1 st from back needle tog with 1 st from front needle; rep from *. Break yarn.**

Bottom Inside of Mouth *Row 1 (RS)* Sl first 11 sts to RH needle, then join B and K6 center sts, W&T.

Row 2 P7, W&T.

Row 3 K8, W&T.

Row 4 P9, W&T. Cont to work 1 more st before W&T every row until last row worked is: K26, W&T.

Next row (WS) P27.

Next row K28.

Next row P28.

Upper Inside of Mouth and Upper Lip Rep from ** to ** once.

Upper Head shaping *Row 1 (RS)* Sl first 11 sts to RH needle, then join MC and K6 center sts, W&T.

Row 2 P7, W&T.

Row 3 K8, W&T.

Row 4 P9, W&T. Cont to work 1 more st before W&T every row until last row worked is: K26, W&T.

Next row (WS) P27.

Next row K28.

Next row P28.

BODY BACK

Work 4 rows even in St st.

SCALES

Row 1 (RS) K17, W&T.

Row 2 P5, W&T.

Row 3 K4, W&T.

Row 4 P3, W&T.

Row 5 K2, W&T.

Row 6 P3, W&T.

Row 7 K4, W&T.

Row 8 P5, W&T.

Row 9 K17.

Row 10 P28.

Row 11 K11, sl 3 sts to cn and hold to back, k3, k3 from cn, k11.

Rows 12 and 14 K28.

Row 13 P28. Rep rows 1-14 for desired number of scales. Finished scales can be lightly stuffed with a bit of tissue or fiberfill to help them stand up.

OPTIONAL STIFFENING:

Younger children may find it easier to manage the puppet with cardboard stiffening in the mouth. Fold a piece of shirt cardboard in half and trace the shape of the mouth onto the cardboard. Cut through both thicknesses to cut out an oval. Insert the folded cardboard into the puppet so that both sides of the mouth are supported.

toy basics

KNITTING NEEDLES		CROCHET HOOKS	
US	**METRIC**	**US**	**METRIC**
0	2mm	14 steel	.60mm
1	2.25mm	12 steel	.75mm
2	2.75mm	10 steel	1.00mm
3	3.25mm	6 steel	1.50mm
4	3.5mm	5 steel	1.75mm
5	3.75mm	B/1	2.25mm
6	4 mm	C/2	2.75mm
7	4.5mm	D/3	3.25mm
8	5mm	E/4	3.50mm
9	5.5mm	F/5	3.75mm
10	6mm	G/6	4.00mm
10½	6.5mm	H/8	5.00mm
11	8mm	I/9	5.50mm
13	9mm	J/10	6.00mm
15	10mm	K/10½	6.50mm
17	12.75mm	L-11	8.00mm
19	15mm		
35	19mm		

You don't have to be a knitting expert to get the hang of the offerings in our collection. In fact, we created this volume for those of you who are just starting to get the hang of clicking your needles, or just want to make something swiftly and comfortably. Either way, these patterns bring an array of ideas and styles right to your fingertips, with plenty of support and clear directions along the way.

All projects feature easy-to-follow instructions and full-page color photographs. Also included is a detailed stitch glossary, comprehensive resource guide and step-by-step illustrations of embroidery stitches.

GAUGE

It is always important to knit a gauge swatch. If a gauge is incorrect, a colorwork pattern may become distorted. The type of needles or hooks used—straight, circular, wood or metal—will influence gauge, so make your swatch with the needles/hooks you plan to use for the project. Measure gauge as illustrated here. (Launder and block your gauge swatch before taking measurements). Try different needle/hook sizes until your sample measures the required number of stitches and rows. To get fewer stitches to the inch/cm, use larger needles/hooks; to get more stitches to the inch/cm, use smaller needles/hooks. It's a good idea to keep your gauge swatch to test any embroidery or embellishment, as well as blocking, and cleaning methods.

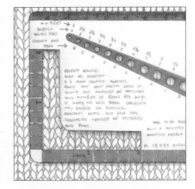

INVISIBLE SEAMING: STOCKINETTE ST

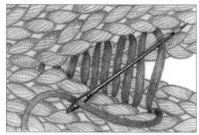

To make an invisible side seam in a garment worked in stockinette stitch, insert tapestry needle under the horizontal bar between the first and second stitches. Insert the needle into the corresponding bar on the other piece. Pull the yarn gently until the sides meet. Then, continue alternating from side to side.

Not only are the projects fun to make, but they will also provide babies and children with hours of enjoyment and entertainment.

Feel free to experiment—now is the time to test out your favorite yarns and colors and try something different. Since these are toys, they're meant to be fanciful and fun. You may just end up creating a new texture or color combination that will surprise you.

DISCLAIMER

While these toys are lovely additions to any child's cache, we would also like to remind you that many of these designs require small parts, such as buttons, that can loosen or fall off. To avoid any accidents, you may want to consider embroidering faces or using alternative decorations for smaller children.

YARN SELECTION

For an exact reproduction of the projects photographed, use the yarn listed in the "Materials" section of the pattern. We've chosen yarns that are readily available in the U.S. and Canada at the time of printing. The Resources list on page 128 provides addresses of yarn distributors. Contact them for the name of a retailer in your area.

YARN SUBSTITUTION

You may wish to try different yarns. Perhaps you view small-scale projects as a chance to incorporate leftovers from your yarn stash, or the yarn specified may not be available in your area. You'll need to knit to the given gauge to obtain the knitted measurements with a substitute yarn (see "Gauge" on page 122). In addition, be sure to consider how the fiber content of the substitute yarn will affect the comfort and the care of your projects.

After you've successfully gauge-swatched a substitute yarn, you'll need to figure out how much of the new yarn the project requires. First, find the total length of the original yarn in the pattern (multiply number of balls by yards/meters per ball). Divide this figure by the new yards/meters per ball (listed on the ball band). Round up to the next whole number. The answer is the number of balls required.

FOLLOWING CHARTS

Charts are a convenient way to follow colorwork and other stitch patterns at a glance. *FCEK* stitch charts utilize the universal knitting language of "symbolcraft." When knitting back and forth in rows, read charts from right to left on right side (RS) rows and from left to right on wrong side (WS) rows, repeating any stitch and row repeats as directed in the pattern. When knitting in the round, read charts from right to left on every round. Posting a self-adhesive note under your working row is an easy way to keep track of your place on a chart.

COLORWORK KNITTING

Two main types of colorwork are explored in this book.

INTARSIA

Intarsia is accomplished with separate bobbins of individual hues. This method is ideal for large blocks of color or for motifs that aren't repeated close together. When changing colors, always pick up the new color and wrap it around the old one to prevent holes.

STRANDING

When motifs are closely placed, colorwork is accomplished by stranding along two or more colors per row, creating "floats" on the wrong side of the fabric. This technique is sometimes called Fair Isle knitting after the traditional Fair

toy basics

Isle patterns that are composed of small motifs with frequent color changes.

To keep an even tension and prevent holes while knitting, pick up yarns alternately over and under one another across or around. While knitting, stretch the stitches on the needle slightly wider than the length of the float at the back to keep work from puckering.

When changing colors at the beginning of rows or rounds, carry yarn along for a few rows only, or cut yarn and rejoin when needed. It is important to keep the "floats" small and neat so they don't catch when pulling on the piece.

CARE

Refer to the yarn label for the recommended cleaning method. Many of the projects in the book can be either washed by hand, or in the machine on a gentle or wool cycle, in luke-warm water with a mild detergent. Do not agitate, or soak for more than 10 minute. Rinse gently with tepid water, then fold in a towel and gently press the water out. Lay flat to dry away from excess heat and light. Check the yarn band for any specific care instructions such as dry cleaning or tumble drying.

CROCHET STITCHES

chain

1 Pass the yarn over the hook and catch it with the hook.

2 Draw the yarn through the loop on the hook.

3 Repeat steps 1 and 2 to make a chain.

single crochet

1 Insert the hook through top two loops of a stitch. Pass the yarn over the hook and draw up a loop—two loops on hook.

2 Pass the yarn over the hook and draw through both loops on hook.

3 Continue in the same way, inserting the hook into each stitch.

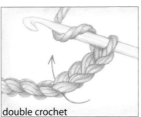

double crochet

1 Pass yarn over hook. Insert hook through the top two loops of a stitch.

2 Pass yarn over hook and draw up a loop—three loops on hook.

3 Pass yarn over hook and draw it through the first two loops on the hook, pass yarn over hook and draw through the remaining two loops. Continue in the same way, inserting hook into each stitch.

DUPLICATE STITCH

Duplicate stitch covers a knit stitch. Bring the needle up below the stitch to be worked. Insert the needle under both loops one row above and pull it through. Insert it back into the stitch below and through the center of the next stitch in one motion, as shown.

TWISTED CORD

1 If you have someone to help you, insert a pencil or knitting needle through each end of the strands. If not, place one end over a doorknob and put a pencil through the other end. Turn the strands clockwise until they are tightly twisted.

2 Keeping the strands taut, fold the piece in half. Remove the pencils and allow the cords to twist onto themselves.

EMBROIDERY STITCHES

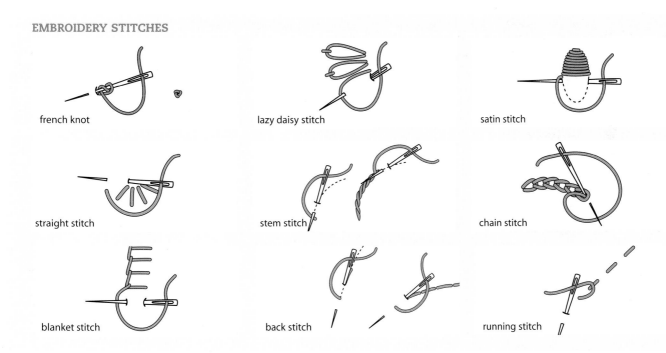

french knot

lazy daisy stitch

satin stitch

straight stitch

stem stitch

chain stitch

blanket stitch

back stitch

running stitch

knit/crochet terms and abbreviations

approx approximately

beg begin(ning)

bind off Used to finish an edge and keep stitches from unraveling. Lift the first stitch over the second, the second over the third, etc. (UK: cast off)

cast on A foundation row of stitches placed on the needle in order to begin knitting.

CC contrast color

ch chain(s)

cm centimeter(s)

cont continu(e)(ing)

dc double crochet (UK: tr–treble)

dec decrease(ing)–Reduce the stitches in a row (knit 2 together).

dpn double-pointed needle(s)

dtr double treble (UK: trtr—triple treble)

foll follow(s)(ing)

g gram(s)

garter stitch Knit every row. Circular knitting: knit one round, then purl one round.

grp(s) group(s)

hdc half double crochet (UK: htr–half treble)

inc increase(ing)–Add stitches in a row (knit into the front and back of a stitch).

k knit

k2tog knit 2 stitches together

LH left-hand

lp(s) loop(s)

m meter(s)

M1 make one stitch–With the needle tip, lift the strand between last stitch worked and next stitch on the left-hand needle and knit into the back of it. One stitch has been added.

MC main color

mm millimeter(s)

no stitch On some charts, "no stitch" is indicated with shaded spaces where stitches have been decreased or not yet made. In such cases, work the stitches of the chart, skipping over the "no stitch" spaces.

oz ounce(s)

p purl

p2tog purl 2 stitches together

pat(s) pattern

pick up and knit (purl) Knit (or purl) into the loops along an edge.

pm place markers–Place or attach a loop of contrast yarn or purchased stitch marker as indicated.

psso pass slip stitch(es) over

rem remain(s)(ing)

rep repeat

rev St st reverse stockinette stitch–Purl right-side rows, knit wrong-side rows. Circular knitting: purl all rounds. (UK: reverse stocking stitch)

rnd(s) round(s)

RH right-hand

RS right side(s)

sc single crochet (UK: dc–double crochet)

sk skip

SKP Slip 1, knit 1, pass slip stitch over knit 1.

SK2P Slip 1, knit 2 together, pass slip stitch over the knit 2 together.

S2KP Slip 2 stitches, knit 1, pass the 2 slipped stitches over knit 1.

sl slip–An unworked stitch made by passing a stitch from the left-hand to the right-hand needle as if to purl.

sl st slip stitch (UK: sc–single crochet)

sp(s) space(s)

ssk slip, slip, knit–Slip next 2 stitches knitwise, one at a time, to right-hand needle. Insert tip of left-hand needle into fronts of these stitches from left to right. Knit them together. One stitch has been decreased.

ssp slip, slip, purl–Slip next 2 stitches purlwise, one at a time, to right-hand needle. Insert tip of left-hand needle into backs of these stitches from left to right. Purl them together. One stitch has been decreased.

sssk Slip next 3 sts knitwise, one at a time, to right-hand needle. Insert tip of left-hand needle into fronts of these stitches from left to right. Knit them together. Two stitches have been decreased.

st(s) stitch(es)

St st Stockinette stitch–Knit right-side rows, purl wrong-side rows. Circular knitting: knit all rounds. (UK: stocking stitch)

tbl through back of loop

t-ch turning chain

tog together

tr treble (UK: dtr—double treble)

trtr triple treble (UK: qtr—quadruple treble)

WS wrong side(s)

wyib with yarn in back

wyif with yarn in front

work even Continue in pattern without increasing or decreasing. (UK: work straight)

yd yard(s)

yo yarn over–Make a new stitch by wrapping the yarn over the right-hand needle. (UK: yfwd, yon, yrn)

* = Repeat directions following * as many times as indicated.

[ ] = Repeat directions inside brackets as many times as indicated.

resources

Bernat®
PO Box 40
Listowel, ON N4W 3H3
Canada

Berroco, Inc.
14 Elmdale Road
PO Box 367
Uxbridge, MA 01569

Brown Sheep Yarn Co.
100662 County Road 16
Mitchell, NE 69357

Caron International
1481 W. 2nd Street
Washington, NC 27889

Cascade Yarns, Inc.
1224 Andover Park E.
Tukwila, WA 98188-3905

Classic Elite Yarns
300A Jackson Ave.
Lowell, MA 01854

Cleckheaton
distributed by
Plymouth Yarns

Coats & Clark
Attn: Consumer Service
PO Box 12229
Greenville, SC 29612-0229
(800) 648-1479

Filatura Di Crosa
distributed by
Tahki•Stacy Charles, Inc.

Lang
distributed by
Berroco, Inc.

Lion Brand Yarns
34 West 15th Street
New York, NY 10011
www.lionbrand.com

Patons®
PO Box 40
Listowel, ON N4W 3H3
Canada

Plymouth Yarns
PO Box 28
Bristol, PA 19007

Tahki•Stacy Charles, Inc.
70-30 80th Street, Building #36
Ridgewood, NY 11385

Tahki Yarns
distributed by
Tahki•Stacy Charles, Inc.

Trendsetter Yarns
16742 Stagg Street
Suite 104
Van Nuys, CA 91406

We have made every effort to ensure the accuracy of the contents of this publication.
We are not responsible for any human or typographic errors.